SESAME AND LILIES.

TWO LECTURES.

SESAME AND LILIES.

Two Lectures

DELIVERED AT MANCHESTER IN 1864.

BY

JOHN RUSKIN, M.A.

1. *OF KINGS' TREASURIES.*
2. *OF QUEENS' GARDENS.*

"ἀπὸ τῆς χαρᾶς αὐτοῦ ὑπάγει, καὶ ἀγοράζει τὸν ἀγρὸν ἐκεῖνον."

NEW YORK:
JOHN WILEY & SON, 535 BROADWAY.
1866.

SESAME AND LILIES.

LECTURE I.—SESAME.

OF KINGS' TREASURIES.

*ἐξ αὐτῆς ἐξελεύσεται ἄρτος, * * * καὶ χῶμα χουσίον.**

I BELIEVE, ladies and gentlemen, that my first duty this evening is to ask your pardon for the ambiguity of title under which the subject of lecture has been announced; and for having endeavoured, as you may ultimately think, to obtain your audience under false pretences. For indeed I am not going to talk of kings, known as regnant, nor of treasuries, understood to contain wealth; but of quite another order of royalty, and material of riches, than those usually acknowledged. And I had even intended to ask your attention for a little while on trust, and (as sometimes one contrives in taking a friend to see a favourite piece of scenery) to hide what I wanted most to show, with such imperfect cunning as I might, until we had unexpectedly reached the best point of view by winding paths. But since my good plain-

* Job xxviii. 5, 6

spoken friend, Canon Anson, has already partly anticipated my reserved "trot for the avenue" in his first advertised title of subject, "How and What to Read;"—and as also I have heard it said, by men practised in public address, that hearers are never so much fatigued as by the endeavour to follow a speaker who gives them no clue to his purpose, I will take the slight mask off at once, and tell you plainly that I want to speak to you about books; and about the way we read them, and could, or should read them. A grave subject, you will say; and a wide one! Yes; so wide that I shall make no effort to touch the compass of it. I will try only to bring before you a few simple thoughts about reading, which press themselves upon me every day more deeply, as I watch the course of the public mind with respect to our daily enlarging means of education, and the answeringly wider spreading, on the levels, of the irrigation of literature. It happens that I have practically some connexion with schools for different classes of youth; and I receive many letters from parents respecting the education of their children. In the mass of these letters, I am always struck by the precedence which the idea of a "position in life" takes above all other thoughts in the parents'—more especially in the mothers'—minds. "The education befitting such and such a *station in life*"—this is the phrase, this the object, always. They never seek, as far as I can make out, an education good in itself: the conception of abstract rightness in training rarely seems reached by the writers. But an education "which shall keep a good coat on my son's back;—an education which shall enable him to ring with confidence the visitors' bell at double-belled doors; —education which shall result ultimately in establishment of a double-belled door to his own house; in a word, which shall lead to advancement in life." It never seems to occur to the parents that there may be an education which, in itself, *is* advancement in Life;—that any other than that may perhaps be advancement in Death; and that this essential education might be more easily got, or given, than they fancy, if they set about it in the right way; while it is for no price, and by no favour, to be got, if they set about it in the wrong.

Indeed, among the ideas most prevalent and effective in the mind of this busiest of countries, I suppose the first—at least that which is confessed with the greatest frankness, and put forward as the fittest stimulus to youthful exertion—is this of "Advancement in life." My main purpose this evening is to determine, with you, what this idea practically includes, and what it should include.

Practically, then, at present, "advancement in life" means becoming conspicuous in life;—obtaining a position which shall be acknowledged by others to be respectable or honourable. We do not understand by this advancement, in general, the mere making of money, but the being known to have made it; not the accomplishment of any great aim, but the being seen to have accomplished it. In a word, we mean the gratification of our thirst for applause. That thirst, if the last infirmity of noble minds, is also the first infirmity of weak ones; and, on the whole, the strongest impulsive influence of average humanity: the greatest efforts of the race have always been traceable to the love of praise, as its greatest catastrophes to the love of pleasure.

I am not about to attack or defend this impulse. I want you only to feel how it lies at the root of effort; especially of all modern effort. It is the gratification of vanity which is, with us, the stimulus of toil, and balm of repose; so closely does it touch the very springs of life, that the wounding of our vanity is always spoken of (and truly) as in its measure *mortal;* we call it "mortification," using the same expression which we should apply to a gangrenous and incurable bodily hurt. And although few of us may be physicians enough to recognise the various effect of this passion upon health and energy, I believe most honest men know, and would at once acknowledge, its leading power with them as a motive. The seaman does not commonly desire to be made captain only because he knows he can manage the ship better than any other sailor on board. He wants to be made captain that he may be *called* captain. The clergyman does not usually want to be made a bishop only because he believes that no other hand can, as firmly as his, direct the diocese through its difficulties. He wants to be made bishop primarily that he may be called "My Lord." And a prince does not usually desire to enlarge, or a subject to gain, a kingdom because he believes that no one else can as well serve the state upon the throne; but, briefly, because he wishes to be addressed as "Your Majesty," by as many lips as may be brought to such utterance.

This, then, being the main idea of advancement in life, the force of it applies, for all of us, according to our station, particularly to that secondary result of such advancement which we call "getting into good society." We want to get into good society, not that we may have it, but that we may be seen in it; and our notion of its goodness depends primarily on its conspicuousness.

Will you pardon me if I pause for a moment to put what I fear you may think an impertinent question? I never can go on with an address unless I feel, or know, that my audience are either with me or against me: (I do not much care which, in beginning;) but I must know where they are; and I would fain find out, at this instant, whether you think I am putting the motives of popular action too low. I am resolved to-night, to state them low enough to be admitted as probable; for whenever, in my writings on Political Economy, I assume that a little honesty, or generosity,—or what used to be called "virtue"—may be calculated upon as a human motive of action, people always answer me, saying, "You must not calculate on that: that is not in human nature: you must not assume anything to be common to men but acquisitiveness and jealousy; no other feeling ever has influence on them, except accidentally, and in matters out of the way of business." I begin accordingly to-night low down in the scale of motives; but I must know if you think me right in doing so. Therefore, let me ask those who admit the love of praise to be usually the strongest motive in men's minds in seeking advancement, and the honest desire of doing any kind of duty to be an entirely secondary one, to hold up their hands. (*About a dozen of hands held up—the audience partly not being sure the lecturer is serious, and partly shy of expressing opinion.*) I am quite serious —I really do want to know what you think; however, I can judge by putting the reverse question. Will those who think that duty is generally the first, and love of praise the second motive, hold up their hands? (*One hand reported to have been held up, behind the lecturer.*) Very good: I see you are with me, and that you think I have not begun too near the ground. Now, without teasing you by putting farther question, I venture to assume that you will admit duty as at least a secondary or tertiary motive. You think that the desire of doing something useful, or obtaining some real good, is indeed an existent collateral idea, though a secondary one, in most men's desire of advancement. You will grant that moderately honest men desire place and office, at least in some measure for the sake of their beneficent power; and would wish to associate rather with sensible and well-informed persons than with fools and ignorant persons, whether they are seen in the company of the sensible ones or not. And finally, without being troubled by repetition of any common truisms about the preciousness of friends, and the influence of companions, you will admit, doubtless, that according to the sincerity of our desire that our friends may be true, and our companions wise,—and in proportion to the earnestness and discretion with which we choose both, will be the general chances of our happiness and usefulness.

But, granting that we had both the will and the sense to choose our friends well, how few of us have the power! or, at least, how limited, for most, is the sphere of choice! Nearly all our associations are determined by chance or necessity; and restricted within a narrow circle. We cannot know whom we would; and those whom we know, we cannot have at our side when we most need them. All the higher circles of human intelligence are, to those beneath, only momentarily and partially open. We may, by good fortune, obtain a glimpse of a great poet, and hear the sound of his voice; or put a question to a man of science, and be answered good-humouredly. We may intrude ten minutes' talk on a cabinet minister, answered probably with words worse than silence, being deceptive; or snatch, once or twice in our lives, the privilege of throwing a bouquet in the path of a Princess, or arresting the kind glance of a Queen. And yet these momentary chances we covet; and spend our years, and passions, and powers in pursuit of little more than these; while, meantime, there is a society continually open to us, of people who will talk to us as long as we like, whatever our rank or occupation;—talk to us in the best words they can choose, and with thanks if we listen to them. And this society, because it is so numerous and so gentle,—and can be kept waiting round us all day long, not to grant audience, but to gain it;—kings and statesmen lingering patiently in those plainly furnished and narrow anterooms, our bookcase shelves,—we make no account of that company,—perhaps never listen to a word they would say, all day long!

You may tell me, perhaps, or think within yourselves, that the apathy with which we regard this company of the noble, who are praying us to listen to them, and the passion with which we pursue the company, probably of the ignoble, who despise us, or who have nothing to teach us, are grounded in this,—that we can see the faces of the living men, and it is themselves, and not their sayings, with which we desire to become familiar. But it is not so. Suppose you never were to see their faces;—suppose you could be put behind a screen in the statesman's cabinet, or the prince's chamber, would you not be glad to listen to their words, though you were forbidden to advance beyond the screen? And when the screen is only a little less, folded in two, instead of four, and you can be hidden behind the cover of the two boards that bind a book, and listen, all day long, not to the casual talk, but to the studied, determined, chosen addresses of the wisest of men;—this station of audience, and honourable privy council, you despise!

But perhaps you will say that it is because the living people talk of things that are passing, and are of immediate interest to you, that you desire to hear them. Nay; that cannot be so, for the living people will themselves tell you about passing matters, much better in their writings than in their careless talk. But I admit that this motive does influence you, so far as you prefer those rapid and ephemeral writings to slow and enduring writings—books, properly so called. For all books are divisible into two classes, the books of the hour, and the books of all time. Mark this distinction—it is not one of quality only. It is not merely the bad book that does not last, and the good one that does. It is a distinction of species. There are good books for the hour, and good ones for all time; bad books for the hour, and bad ones for all time. I must define the two kinds before I go farther.

The good book of the hour, then,—I do not speak of the bad ones—is simply the useful or pleasant talk of some person whom you cannot otherwise converse with, printed for you. Very useful often, telling you what you need to know; very pleasant often, as a sensible friend's present talk would be. These bright accounts of travels; good-humoured and witty discussions of question; lively or pathetic story-telling in the form of novel; firm fact-telling, by the real agents concerned in the events of passing history;—all these books of the hour, multiplying among us as education becomes more general, are a peculiar characteristic and possession of the present age: we ought to be entirely thankful for them, and entirely ashamed of ourselves if we make no good use of them. But we make the worst possible use, if we allow them to usurp the place of true books: for, strictly speaking, they are not books at all, but merely letters or newspapers in good print. Our friend's letter may be delightful, or necessary, to-day: whether worth keeping or not, is to be considered. The newspaper may be entirely proper at breakfast time, but assuredly it is not reading for all day. So, though bound up in a volume, the long letter which gives you so pleasant an account of the inns, and roads, and weather last year at such a place, or which tells you that amusing story, or gives you the real circumstances of such and such events, however valuable for occasional reference, may not be, in the real sense of the word, a "book" at all, nor, in the real sense, to be "read." A book is essentially not a talked thing, but a written thing; and written, not with the view of mere communication, but of permanence. The book of talk is printed only because its author cannot speak to thousands of people at once; if he could, he would—the volume is mere *multiplication* of his voice. You cannot talk to your friend in India; if you could, you would; you write instead: that is mere *conveyance* of voice. But a book is written, not to multiply the voice merely, not to carry it merely, but to preserve it. The author has something to say which he perceives to be true and useful, or helpfully beautiful. So far as he knows, no one has yet said it; so far as he knows, no one else can say it. He is bound to say it, clearly and melodiously if he may; clearly, at all events. In the sum of his life he finds this to be the thing, or group of things, manifest to him;—this the piece of true knowledge, or sight, which his share of sunshine and earth has permitted him to seize. He would fain set it down for ever; engrave it on rock, if he could; saying, "This is the best of me; for the rest, I ate, and drank, and slept, loved, and hated, like another; my life was as the vapour, and is not; but this I saw and knew: this, if anything of mine, is worth your memory." That is his "writing;" it is, in his small human way, and with whatever degree of true inspiration is in him, his inscription, or scripture. That is a "Book."

Perhaps you think no books were ever so written?

But, again, I ask you, do you at all believe in honesty, or at all in kindness? or do you think there is never any honesty or benevolence in wise people? None of us, I hope, are so unhappy as to think that. Well, whatever bit of a wise man's work is honestly and benevolently done, that bit is his book, or his piece of art. It is mixed always with evil fragments—ill-done, redundant, affected work. But if you read rightly, you will easily discover the true bits, and those *are* the book.

Now books of this kind have been written in all ages by their greatest men;—by great leaders, great statesmen, and great thinkers. These are all at your choice; and life is short. You have heard as much before;—yet have you measured and mapped out this short life and its possibilities? Do you know, if you read this, that you cannot read that—that what you lose to-day you cannot gain to-morrow? Will you go and gossip with your housemaid, or your stable-boy, when you may talk with queens and kings; or flatter yourselves that it is with any worthy consciousness of your own claims to respect that you jostle with the common crowd for *entrée* here, and audience there, when all the while this eternal court is open to you, with its society wide as the world, multitudinous as its days, the chosen, and the mighty, of every place and time? Into that you may enter always; in that you may take fellowship and rank according to your wish; from that, once entered into it, you can never be outcast but by your own fault; by your aristocracy of companionship there, your own inherent aristocracy will be assuredly tested, and the motives with which you strive to take high place in the society of the living, measured, as to all the truth and sincerity that are in them, by the place you desire to take in this company of the Dead.

"The place you desire," and the place you *fit yourself for*, I must also say; because, observe, this court of the past differs from all living aristocracy in this:—it is open to labour and to merit, but to nothing else. No wealth will bribe, no name overawe, no artifice deceive, the guardian of those Elysian gates. In the deep sense, no vile or vulgar person ever enters there. At the portières of that silent Faubourg St. Germain, there is but brief question, "Do you deserve to enter?" "Pass. Do you ask to be the companion of nobles? Make yourself noble, and you shall be. Do you long for the conversation of the wise? Learn to understand it, and you shall hear it. But on other terms ?—no. If you will not rise to us, we cannot stoop to you. The living lord may assume courtesy, the living philosopher explain his thought to you with considerable pain; but here we neither feign nor interpret; you must rise to the level of our thoughts if you would be gladdened by them, and share our feelings, if you would recognise our presence."

This, then, is what you have to do, and I admit that it is much. You must, in a word, love these people, if you are to be among them. No ambition is of any use. They scorn your ambition. You must love them, and show your love in these two following ways.

I.—First, by a true desire to be taught by them, and to enter into their thoughts. To enter into theirs, observe; not to find your own expressed by them. If the person who wrote the book is not wiser than you, you need not read it; if he be, he will think differently from you in many respects.

Very ready we are to say of a book, "How good this is—that's exactly what I think!" But the right feeling is, "How strange that is! I never thought of that before, and yet I see it is true; or if I do not now, I hope I shall, some day." But whether thus submissively or not, at least be sure that you go to the author to get at *his* meaning, not to find yours. Judge it afterwards, if you think yourself qualified to do so;

but ascertain it first. And be sure also, if the author is worth anything, that you will not get at his meaning all at once;—nay, that at his whole meaning you will not for a long time arrive in any wise. Not that he does not say what he means, and in strong words too; but he cannot say it all; and what is more strange, will not, but in a hidden way and in parables, in order that he may be sure you want it. I cannot quite see the reason of this, nor analyse that cruel reticence in the breasts of wise men which makes them always hide their deeper thought. They do not give it you by way of help, but of reward, and will make themselves sure that you deserve it before they allow you to reach it. But it is the same with the physical type of wisdom, gold. There seems, to you and me, no reason why the electric forces of the earth should not carry whatever there is of gold within it at once to the mountain tops, so that kings and people might know that all the gold they could get was there; and without any trouble of digging, or anxiety, or chance, or waste of time, cut it away, and coin as much as they needed. But Nature does not manage it so. She puts it in little fissures in the earth, nobody knows where: you may dig long and find none; you must dig painfully to find any.

And it is just the same with men's best wisdom. When you come to a good book, you must ask yourself, "Am I inclined to work as an Australian miner would? Are my pickaxes and shovels in good order, and am I in good trim myself, my sleeves well up to the elbow, and my breath good, and my temper?" And, keeping the figure a little longer, even at cost of tiresomeness, for it is a thoroughly useful one, the metal you are in search of being the author's mind or meaning, his words are as the rock which you have to crush and smelt in order to get at it. And your pickaxes are your own care, wit, and learning; your smelting-furnace is your own thoughtful soul. Do not hope to get at any good author's meaning without those tools and that fire; often you will need sharpest, finest chiselling, and patientest fusing, before you can gather one grain of the metal.

And, therefore, first of all, I tell you, earnestly and authoritatively, (I *know* I am right in this,) you must get into the habit of looking intensely at words, and assuring yourself of their meaning, syllable by syllable—nay, letter by letter. For though it is only by reason of the opposition of letters in the function of signs, to sounds in function of signs, that the study of books is called "literature," and that a man versed in it is called, by the consent of nations, a man of letters instead of a man of books, or of words, you may yet connect with that accidental nomenclature this real principle: —that you might read all the books in the British Museum (if you could live long enough), and remain an utterly "illiterate," uneducated person; but that if you read ten pages of a good book, letter by letter,—that is to say, with real accuracy,—you are for evermore in some measure an educated person. The entire difference between education and non-education (as regards the merely intellectual part of it), consists in this accuracy. A well-educated gentleman may not know many languages,—may not be able to speak any but his own,—may have read very few books. But whatever language he knows, he knows precisely; whatever word he pronounces he pronounces rightly; above all, he is learned in the *peerage* of words; knows the words of true descent and ancient blood, at a glance, from words of modern canaille; remembers all their ancestry—their intermarriages, distantest relationships, and the extent to which they were admitted, and offices they held, among the national noblesse of words at any time, and in any country. But an uneducated person may know by memory any number of languages, and talk them all, and yet truly know not a word of any,—not a word even of his own. An ordinarily clever and sensible seaman will be able to make his way ashore at most ports; yet he has only to speak a sentence of any language to be known for an illiterate person: so also the accent, or turn of expression of a single sentence will at once mark a scholar. And this is so strongly felt, so conclusively admitted by educated persons, that a false accent or a mistaken syllable is enough, in the parliament of any civilized nation, to assign to a man a certain degree of inferior standing for ever. And this is right; but it is a pity that the accuracy insisted on is not greater, and required to a serious purpose. It is right that a false Latin quantity should excite a smile in the House of Commons; but it is wrong that a false English meaning should *not* excite a frown there. Let the accent of words be watched, by all means, but let their meaning be watched more closely still, and fewer will do the work. A few words well chosen and well distinguished, will do work that a thousand cannot, when every one is acting, equivocally, in the function of another. Yes; and words, if they are not watched, will do deadly work sometimes. There are masked words droning and skulking about us in Europe just now,—(there never were so many, owing to the spread of a shallow, blotching, blundering, infectious "information," or rather deformation, everywhere, and to the teaching of catechisms and phrases at schools instead of human meanings)—there are masked words abroad, I say, which nobody understands, but which everybody uses, and most people will also fight for, live for, or even die for, fancying they mean this, or that, or the other, of things dear to them: for such words wear chamæleon cloaks—"groundlion" cloaks, of the colour of the ground of any man's fancy: on that ground they lie in wait, and rend him with a spring from it. There were never creatures of prey so mischievous, never diplomatists so cunning, never poisoners so deadly, as these masked words; they are the unjust stewards of all men's ideas: whatever fancy or favourite instinct a man most cherishes, he gives to his favourite masked word to take care of for him; the word at last comes to have an infinite power over him,—you cannot get at him but by its ministry. And in languages so mongrel in breed as the English, there is a fatal power of equivocation put into men's hands, almost whether they will or no, in being able to use Greek or Latin forms for a word when they want it to be respectable, and Saxon or otherwise common forms when they want to discredit it. What a singular and salutary effect, for instance, would be produced on the minds of people who are in the habit of taking the Form of the words they live by, for the Power of which those words tell them, if we always either retained, or refused, the Greek form "biblos," or "biblion," as the right expression for "book"—instead of employing it only in the one instance in which we wish to give dignity to the idea, and translating it everywhere else. How wholesome it would be for the many simple persons who worship the Letter of God's Word instead of its Spirit, (just as other idolaters worship His picture instead of His presence,) if, in such places (for instance) as Acts xix. 19 we retained the Greek expression, instead of translating it, and they had to read—"Many of them also which used curious arts, brought their bibles together, and burnt them before all men; and they counted the price of them, and found it fifty thousand pieces of silver!" Or if, on the other hand, we translated instead of retaining it, and always spoke of "the Holy Book," instead of "Holy Bible," it might come into more heads than it does at present that the Word of God, by which the heavens were, of old, and by which they are now kept in store,* cannot be made a present of to anybody in morocco binding; nor sown on any wayside by help either of steam plough or steam press; but is nevertheless being offered to us daily, and by us with contumely refused; and sown in us daily, and by us as instantly as may be, choked.

So, again, consider what effect has been produced on the English vulgar mind by the use of the sonorous Latin form "damno," in translating the Greek κατακρίνω, when people charitably wish to make it forcible; and the substitution of the temperate "condemn" for it, when they choose to keep it gentle. And what notable sermons have been preached by illiterate clergymen on—"He that believeth not shall be damned;" though they would shrink with horror from translating Heb. xi. 7, "The saving of his house, by which he damned the world," or John viii. 12, "Woman, hath no man damned thee? She saith, No man, Lord. Jesus answered her, Neither do I damn thee; go and sin no more." And

* 2 Peter iii. 5—7.

divisions in the mind of Europe, which have cost seas of blood, and in the defence of which the noblest souls of men have been cast away in frantic desolation, countless as forest-leaves—though, in the heart of them, founded on deeper causes—have nevertheless been rendered practicably possible, mainly, by the European adoption of the Greek word for a public meeting, to give peculiar respectability to such meetings, when held for religious purposes; and other collateral equivocations, such as the vulgar English one of using the word "priest" as a contraction for "presbyter."

Now, in order to deal with words rightly, this is the habit you must form. Nearly every word in your language has been first a word of some other language—of Saxon, German, French, Latin, or Greek; (not to speak of eastern and primitive dialects.) And many words have been all these;—that is to say, have been Greek first, Latin next, French or German next, and English last: undergoing a certain change of sense and use on the lips of each nation; but retaining a deep vital meaning which all good scholars feel in employing them, even at this day. If you do not know the Greek alphabet, learn it; young or old—girl or boy—whoever you may be, if you think of reading seriously (which, of course, implies that you have some leisure at command), learn your Greek alphabet; then get good dictionaries of all these languages, and whenever you are in doubt about a word, hunt it down patiently. Read Max Müller's lectures thoroughly, to begin with; and, after that, never let a word escape you that looks suspicious. It is severe work; but you will find it, even at first, interesting, and at last, endlessly amusing. And the general gain to your character, in power and precision, will be quite incalculable.

Mind, this does not imply knowing, or trying to know, Greek, or Latin, or French. It takes a whole life to learn any language perfectly. But you can easily ascertain the meanings through which the English word has passed; and those which in a good writer's work it must still bear.

And now, merely for example's sake, I will, with your permission, read a few lines of a true book with you, carefully; and see what will come out of them. I will take a book perfectly known to you all; No English words are more familiar to us, yet nothing perhaps has been less read with sincerity. I will take these few following lines of Lycidas.

"Last came, and last did go,
The pilot of the Galilean lake;
Two massy keys he bore of metals twain,
(The golden opes, the iron shuts amain),
He shook his mitred locks, and stern bespake,
How well could I have spar'd for thee, young swain,
Enow of such as for their bellies' sake
Creep and intrude, and climb into the fold!

Of other care they little reckoning make,
Than how to scramble at the shearers' feast,
And shove away the worthy bidden guest;
Blind mouths! that scarce themselves know how to hold
A sheep-hook, or have learn'd aught else, the least
That to the faithful herdsman's art belongs!
What recks it them? What need they? They are sped;
And when they list, their lean and flashy songs
Grate on their scrannel pipes of wretched straw;
The hungry sheep look up, and are not fed,
But swoln with wind, and the rank mist they draw,
Rot inwardly, and foul contagion spread;
Besides what the grim wolf with privy paw
Daily devours apace, and nothing said."

Let us think over this passage, and examine its words.

First, is it not singular to find Milton assigning to St. Peter, not only his full episcopal function, but the very types of it which Protestants usually refuse most passionately? His "mitred" locks! Milton was no Bishop-lover; how comes St. Peter to be "mitred?" "Two massy keys he bore." Is this, then, the power of the keys claimed by the Bishops of Rome, and is it acknowledged here by Milton only in a poetical licence, for the sake of its picturesqueness, that he may get the gleam of the golden keys to help his effect? Do not think it. Great men do not play stage tricks with doctrines of life and death: only little men do that. Milton means what he says; and means it with his might too—is going to put the whole strength of his spirit presently into the saying of it. For though not a lover of false bishops, he *was* a lover of true ones; and the Lake-pilot is here, in his thoughts, the type and head of true episcopal power. For Milton reads that text, "I will give unto thee the keys of the kingdom of Heaven" quite honestly. Puritan though he be, he would not blot it out of the book because there have been bad bishops; nay, in order to understand him, we must understand that verse first; it will not do to eye it askance, or whisper it under our breath, as if it were a weapon of an adverse sect. It is a solemn, universal assertion, deeply to be kept in mind by all sects. But perhaps we shall be better able to reason on it if we go on a little farther, and come back to it. For clearly, this marked insistance on the power of the true episcopate is to make us feel more weightily what is to be charged against the false claimants of episcopate; or generally, against false claimants of power and rank in the body of the clergy; they who, "for their bellies' sake, creep, and intrude, and climb into the fold."

Do not think Milton uses those three words to fill up his verse, as a loose writer would. He needs all the three; specially those three, and no more than those—"creep," and "intrude," and "climb;" no other words would or could serve the turn, and no more could be added. For they exhaustively comprehend the three classes, correspondent to the three characters, of men who dishonestly seek ecclesiastical power. First, those who "*creep*" into the fold; who do not care for office, nor name, but for secret influence, and do all things occultly and cunningly, consenting to any servility of office or conduct, so only that they may intimately discern, and unawares direct, the minds of men. Then those who "intrude" (thrust, that is) themselves into the fold, who by natural insolence of heart, and stout eloquence of tongue, and fearlessly perseverant self-assertion, obtain hearing and authority with the common crowd. Lastly, those who "climb," who, by labour and learning, both stout and sound, but selfishly exerted in the cause of their own ambition, gain high dignities and authorities, and become "lords over the heritage," though not "ensamples to the flock."

Now go on:—

> "Of other care they little reckoning make,
> Than how to scramble at the shearers' feast.
> *Blind mouths—*"

I pause again, for this is a strange expression; a broken metaphor, one might think, careless and unscholarly.

Not so: its very audacity and pithiness are intended to

make us look close at the phrase and remember it. Those two monosyllables express the precisely accurate contraries of right character, in the two great offices of the Church—those of bishop and pastor.

A Bishop means a person who sees.

A Pastor means one who feeds.

The most unbishoply character a man can have is therefore to be Blind.

The most unpastoral is, instead of feeding, to want to be fed,—to be a Mouth.

Take the two reverses together, and you have "blind mouths." We may advisably follow out this idea a little. Nearly all the evils in the Church have arisen from bishops desiring *power* more than *light*. They want authority, not outlook. Whereas their real office is not to rule; though it may be vigorously to exhort and rebuke; it is the king's office to rule; the bishop's office is to *oversee* the flock; to number it, sheep by sheep; to be ready always to give full account of it. Now it is clear he cannot give account of the souls, if he has not so much as numbered the bodies of his flock. The first thing, therefore, that a bishop has to do is at least to put himself in a position in which, at any moment, he can obtain the history from childhood of every living soul in his diocese, and of its present state. Down in that back street, Bill, and Nancy, knocking each other's teeth out!—

Does the bishop know all about it? Has he his eye upon them? Has he *had* his eye upon them? Can he circumstantially explain to us how Bill got into the habit of beating Nancy about the head? If he cannot, he is no bishop, though he had a mitre as high as Salisbury steeple; he is no bishop,—he has sought to be at the helm instead of the masthead; he has no sight of things. "Nay," you say, it is not his duty to look after Bill in the back street. What! the fat sheep that have full fleeces—you think it is only those he should look after, while (go back to your Milton) "the hungry sheep look up, and are not fed, besides what the grim wolf, with privy paw" (bishops knowing nothing about it) "daily devours apace, and nothing said?"

"But that's not our idea of a bishop." Perhaps not; but it was St. Paul's; and it was Milton's. They may be right, or we may be; but we must not think we are reading either one or the other by putting our meaning into their words.

I go on.

> "But, swollen with wind, and the rank mist they draw."

This is to meet the vulgar answer that "if the poor are not looked after in their bodies, they are in their souls; they have spiritual food."

And Milton says, "They have no such thing as spiritual

food; they are only swollen with wind." At first you may think that is a coarse type, and an obscure one. But again, it is a quite literally accurate one. Take up your Latin and Greek dictionaries, and find out the meaning of "Spirit." It is only a contraction of the Latin word "breath," and an indistinct translation of the Greek word for "wind." The same word is used in writing, "The wind bloweth where it listeth;" and in writing, "So is every one that is born of the Spirit;" born of the *breath*, that is; for it means the breath of God, in soul and body. We have the true sense of it in our words "inspiration" and "expire." Now, there are two kinds of breath with which the flock may be filled; God's breath, and man's. The breath of God is health, and life, and peace to them, as the air of heaven is to the flocks on the hills; but man's breath—the word which *he* calls spiritual,—is disease and contagion to them, as the fog of the fen. They rot inwardly with it; they are puffed up by it, as a dead body by the vapours of its own decomposition. This is literally true of all false religious teaching; the first, and last, and fatalest sign of it is that "puffing up." Your converted children, who teach their parents; your converted convicts, who teach honest men; your converted dunces, who, having lived in cretinous stupefaction half their lives, suddenly awaking to the fact of there being a God, fancy themselves therefore His peculiar people and messengers;

your sectarians of every species, small and great, Catholic or Protestant, of high church or low, in so far as they think themselves exclusively in the right and others wrong; and pre-eminently, in every sect, those who hold that men can be saved by thinking rightly instead of doing rightly, by word instead of act, and wish instead of work:—these are the true fog children—clouds, these, without water; bodies, these, of putrescent vapour and skin, without blood or flesh: blown bag-pipes for the fiends to pipe with—corrupt, and corrupting,—"Swollen with wind, and the rank mist they draw."

Lastly, let us return to the lines respecting the power of the keys, for now we can understand them. Note the difference between Milton and Dante in their interpretation of this power: for once, the latter is weaker in thought; he supposes *both* the keys to be of the gate of heaven; one is of gold, the other of silver: they are given by St. Peter to the sentinel angel; and it is not easy to determine the meaning either of the substances of the three steps of the gate, or of the two keys. But Milton makes one, of gold, the key of heaven; the other, of iron, the key of the prison, in which the wicked teachers are to be bound who "have taken away the key of knowledge, yet entered not in themselves."

We have seen that the duties of bishop and pastor are to see, and feed; and, of all who do so, it is said, "He that watereth, shall be watered also himself." But the reverse is truth also. He that watereth not, shall be *withered* himself; and he that seeth not, shall himself be shut out of sight,—shut into the perpetual prison-house. And that prison opens here, as well as hereafter: he who is to be bound in heaven must first be bound on earth. That command to the strong angels, of which the rock-apostle is the image, "Take him, and bind him hand and foot, and cast him out," issues, in its measure, against the teacher, for every help withheld, and for every truth refused, and for every falsehood enforced; so that he is more strictly fettered the more he fetters, and farther outcast, as he more and more misleads, till at last the bars of the iron cage close upon him, and as "the golden opes, the iron shuts amain."

We have got something out of the lines, I think, and much more is yet to be found in them; but we have done enough by way of example of the kind of word-by-word examination of your author which is rightly called "reading;" watching every accent and expression, and putting ourselves always in the author's place, annihilating our own personality, and seeking to enter into his, so as to be able assuredly to say, "Thus Milton thought," not "Thus I thought, in mis-reading Milton." And by this process you will gradually come to attach less weight to your own "Thus I thought" at other times. You will begin to perceive that what *you* thought was a matter of no serious importance;—that your thoughts on any subject are not perhaps the clearest and wisest that could be arrived at thereupon:—in fact, that unless you are a very singular person, you cannot be said to have any "thoughts" at all; that you have no materials for them, in any serious matters;—no right to "think," but only to try to learn more of the facts. Nay, most probably all your life (unless, as I said, you are a singular person) you will have no legitimate right to an "opinion" on any business, except that instantly under your hand. What must of necessity be done, you can always find out, beyond question, how to do. Have you a house to keep in order, a commodity to sell, a field to plough, a ditch to cleanse? There need be no two opinions about these proceedings; it is at your peril if you have not much more than an "opinion" on the way to manage such matters. And also, outside of your own business, there are one or two subjects on which you are bound to have but one opinion. That roguery and lying are objectionable, and are instantly to be flogged out of the way whenever discovered;—that covetousness and love of quarrelling are dangerous dispositions even in children, and deadly dispositions in men and nations;—that in the end, the God of heaven and earth loves active, modest, and kind people, and hates idle, proud, greedy, and cruel ones;—on these general facts you are bound to have but one, and that a very strong, opinion. For the rest, respecting religious, governments, sciences, arts, you will find that, on the whole, you can know NOTHING,—judge nothing; that the best you can do, even though you may be a well-educated person, is to be silent, and strive to be wiser every day, and to understand a little more of the thoughts of others, which so soon as you try to do honestly, you will discover that the thoughts even of the wisest are very little more than pertinent questions. To put the difficulty into a clear shape, and exhibit to you the grounds for *in*decision, that is all they can generally do for you!—and well for them and for us, if indeed they are able "to mix the music with our thoughts, and sadden us with heavenly doubts." This writer, from whom I have been reading to you, is not among the first or wisest: he sees shrewdly as far as he sees, and therefore it is easy to find out his full meaning, but with the greater men, you cannot fathom their meaning; they do not even wholly measure it themselves,—it is so wide. Suppose I had asked you, for instance, to seek for Shakespeare's opinion, instead of Milton's, on this matter of Church authority?—or for Dante's? Have any of you, at this instant, the least idea what either thought about it? Have you ever balanced the scene with the bishops in Richard III. against the character of Cranmer? the description of St. Francis and St. Dominic against that of him who made Virgil wonder to gaze upon him,—"disteso, tanto vilmente, nell' eterno esilio;" or of him whom Dante stood beside, "come 'l frate che confessa lo perfido assassin?"* Shakespeare and Alighieri knew men better than most of us, I presume! They were both in the midst of the main struggle between the temporal and spiritual powers. They had an opinion, we may guess? But where is it? Bring it into court! Put Shakespeare's or Dante's creed into articles, and send *that* up into the Ecclesiastical Courts!

You will not be able, I tell you again, for many and many a day, to come at the real purposes and teaching of these great men; but a very little honest study of them will enable you to perceive that what you took for your own "judgment" was mere chance prejudice, and drifted, helpless, entangled weed of castaway thought: nay, you will see that most men's minds are indeed little better than rough heath wilderness, neglected and stubborn, partly barren, partly overgrown with pestilent brakes and venomous wind-sown herbage of evil surmise; that the first thing you have to do for them, and yourself, is eagerly and scornfully to set fire to *this*; burn all the jungle into wholesome ash-heaps, and then plough and sow. All the true literary work before you, for life, must begin with obedience to that order, "Break up your fallow ground, and *sow not among thorns*."

II. Having then faithfully listened to the great teachers,

* Inf. xix. 71; xxiii. 117.

that you may enter into their Thoughts, you have yet this higher advance to make;—you have to enter into their Hearts. As you go to them first for clear sight, so you must stay with them that you may share at last their just and mighty Passion. Passion, or "sensation." I am not afraid of the word; still less of the thing. You have heard many outcries against sensation lately; but, I can tell you, it is not less sensation we want, but more. The ennobling difference between one man and another,—between one animal and another,—is precisely in this, that one feels more than another. If we were sponges, perhaps sensation might not be easily got for us; if we were earth-worms, liable at every instant to be cut in two by the spade, perhaps too much sensation might not be good for us. But, being human creatures, *it is* good for us; nay, we are only human in so far as we are sensitive, and our honour is precisely in proportion to our passion.

You know I said of that great and pure society of the dead, that it would allow "no vain or vulgar person to entei there." What do you think I meant by a "vulgar" person? What do you yourselves mean by "vulgarity?" You will find it a fruitful subject of thought; but, briefly, the essence of all vulgarity lies in want of sensation. Simple and innocent vulgarity is merely an untrained and undeveloped bluntness of body and mind; but in true inbred vulgarity, there is a deathful callousness, which, in extremity, becomes capable of every sort of bestial habit and crime, without fear, without pleasure, without horror, and without pity. It is in the blunt hand and the dead heart, in the diseased habit, in the hardened conscience, that men become vulgar; they are for ever vulgar, precisely in proportion as they are incapable of sympathy,—of quick understanding,—of all that, in deep insistance on the common, but most accurate term, may be called the "tact" or touch-faculty of body and soul: that tact which the Mimosa has in trees, which the pure woman has above all creatures;—fineness and fulness of sensation, beyond reason;—the guide and sanctifier of reason itself. Reason can but determine what is true:—it is the God-given passion of humanity which alone can recognise what God has made good.

We come then to that great concourse of the Dead, not merely to know from them what is True, but chiefly to feel with them what is Righteous. Now, to feel with them, we must be like them; and none of us can become that without pains. As the true knowledge is disciplined and tested knowledge,—not the first thought that comes,—so the true passion is disciplined and tested passion—not the first passion that comes. The first that come are the vain, the false, the treacherous; if you yield to them they will lead you wildly and far, in vain pursuit, in hollow enthusiasm, till you have no true purpose and no true passion left. Not that any feeling possible to humanity is in itself wrong, but only wrong when undisciplined. Its nobility is in its force and justice; it is wrong when it is weak, and felt for paltry cause. There is a mean wonder as of a child who sees a juggler tossing golden balls, and this is base, if you will. But do you think that the wonder is ignoble, or the sensation less, with which every human soul is called to watch the golden balls of heaven tossed through the night by the Hand that made them? There is a mean curiosity, as of a child opening a forbidden door, or a servant prying into her master's business;—and a noble curiosity, questioning, in the front of danger, the source of the great river beyond the sand—the place of the great continents beyond the sea;—a nobler curiosity still, which questions of the source of the River of Life, and of the space of the Continent of Heaven,—things which "the angels desire to look into." So the anxiety is ignoble, with which you linger over the course and catastrophe of an idle tale; but do you think the anxiety is less, or greater, with which you watch, or *ought* to watch, the dealings of fate and destiny with the life of an agonised nation? Alas! it is the narrowness, selfishness, minuteness, of your sensation that you have to deplore in England at this day;—sensation which spends itself in bouquets and speeches; in revellings and junketings; in sham fights and gay puppet shows, while you can look on and see noble nations murdered, man by man, woman by woman, child by child, without an effort, or a tear.

I said "minuteness" and "selfishness" of sensation, but in a word, I ought to have said "injustice" or "unrighteousness" of sensation. For as in nothing is a gentleman better to be discerned from a vulgar person, so in nothing is a gentle nation (such nations have been) better to be discerned from a mob, than in this,—that their feelings are constant and just, results of due contemplation, and of equal thought. You can talk a mob into anything; its feelings may be—usually are—on the whole generous and right; but it has no foundation for them, no hold of them; you may tease or tickle it into any, at your pleasure; it thinks by infection, for the most part, catching a passion like a cold, and there is nothing so little that it will not roar itself wild about, when the fit is on;—nothing so great but it will forget in an hour, when the fit is past. But a gentleman's, or a gentle nation's, passions are just, measured, and continuous. A great nation, for instance, does not spend its entire national wits for a couple of months in weighing evidence of a single ruffian's having done a single murder; and for a couple of years, see its own children murder each other by their thousands or tens of thousands a day, considering only what the effect is likely to be on the price of cotton, and caring nowise to determine which side of battle is in the wrong. Neither does a great nation send its poor little boys to jail for stealing six walnuts; and allow its bankrupts to steal their hundreds of thousands with a bow, and its bankers, rich with poor men's savings, to close their doors "under circumstances over which they have no control," with a "by your leave;" and large landed estates to be bought by men who have made their money by going with armed steamers up and down the China Seas, selling opium at the cannon's mouth, and altering, for the benefit of the foreign nation, the common highwayman's demand of "your money *or* your life," into that of "your money *and* your life." Neither does a great nation allow the lives of its innocent poor to be parched out of them by fog fever, and rotted out of them by dunghill plague, for the sake of sixpence a life extra per week to its landlords;* and then debate, with drivelling

* See the evidence in the Medical officer's report to the Privy Council, just published. There are suggestions in its preface which will make some stir among us, I fancy, respecting which let me note these points following:—

There are two theories on the subject of land now abroad, and in contention; both false.

The first is that by Heavenly law, there have always existed, and must tears, and diabolical sympathies, whether it ought not piously to save, and nursingly cherish, the lives of its

continue to exist, a certain number of hereditarily sacred persons, to whom the earth, air, and water of the world belong, as personal property; of which earth, air, and water these persons may, at their pleasure, permit, or forbid, the rest of the human race to eat, to breathe, or to drink. This theory is not for many years longer tenable. The adverse theory is that a division of the land of the world among the mob of the world would immediately elevate the said mob into sacred personages; that houses would then build themselves, and corn grow of itself; and that everybody would be able to live, without doing any work for his living. This theory would also be found highly untenable in practice.

It will, however, require some rough experiments, and rougher catastrophes, even in this magnesium-lighted epoch, before the generality of persons will be convinced that no law concerning anything, least of all concerning land, for either holding or dividing it, or renting it high, or renting it low, would be of the smallest ultimate use to the people, so long as the general contest for life, and for the means of life, remains one of mere brutal competition. That contest, in an unprincipled nation, will take one deadly form or another, whatever laws you make for it. For instance, it would be an entirely wholesome law for England, if it could be carried, that maximum limits should be assigned to incomes, according to classes; and that every nobleman's income should be paid to him as a fixed salary or pension by the nation; and not squeezed by him in a variable sum, at discretion, out of the tenants of his land. But if you could get such a law passed to-morrow; and if, which would be farther necessary, you could fix the value of the assigned incomes by making a murderers. Also, a great nation having made up its mind that hanging is quite the wholesomest process for its

given weight of pure wheat-flour legal tender for a given sum, a twelvemonth would not pass before another currency would have been tacitly established, and the power of accumulative wealth would have re-asserted itself in some other article, or some imaginary sign. Forbid men to buy each other's lives for sovereigns, and they will for shells, or slates. There is only one cure for public distress—and that is public education, directed to make men thoughtful, merciful, and just. There are, indeed, many laws conceivable which would gradually better and strengthen the national temper; but, for the most part, they are such as the national temper must be much bettered before it would bear. A nation in its youth may be helped by laws, as a weak child by backboards, but when it is old, it cannot that way straighten its crooked spine.

And besides, the problem of land, at its worst, is a bye one; distribute the earth as you will, the principal question remains inexorable,—Who is to dig it? Which of us, in brief words, is to do the hard and dirty work for the rest—and for what pay? Who is to do the pleasant and clean work, and for what pay? Who is to do no work, and for what pay? And there are curious moral and religious questions connected with these. How far is it lawful to suck a portion of the soul out of a great many persons, in order to put the abstracted psychical quantities together, and make one very beautiful or ideal soul? If we had to deal with mere blood, instead of spirit, and the thing might literally be done (as it has been done with infants before now) so that it were possible, by taking a certain quantity of blood from the arms of a given number of the mob, and putting it all into one person, to make a more azure-blooded gentleman of him, the thing homicides in general, can yet with mercy distinguish between the degrees of guilt in homicides; and does not yelp like a pack of frost-pinched wolf-cubs on the blood-track of an unhappy crazed boy, or grey-haired clodpate Othello, "perplexed i' the extreme," at the very moment that it is sending a Minister of the Crown to make polite speeches to a man who is bayoneting young girls in their father's sight, and killing noble youths in cool blood, faster than a country butcher kills lambs in spring. And, lastly, a great nation does not mock Heaven and its Powers, by

would of course be managed; but secretly, I should conceive. But now, because it is brain and soul that we abstract, not visible blood, it can be done quite openly; and we live, we gentlemen, on delicatest prey, after the manner of weasels; that is to say, we keep a certain number of clowns digging and ditching, and generally stupified, in order that we, being fed gratis, may have all the thinking and feeling to ourselves. Yet there is a great deal to be said for this. A highly-bred and trained English, French, Austrian, or Italian gentleman (much more a lady) is a great production; a better production than most statues; being beautifully coloured as well as shaped, and plus all the brains; a glorious thing to look at, a wonderful thing to talk to; and you cannot have it, any more than a pyramid or a church, but by sacrifice of much contributed life. And it is, perhaps, better to build a beautiful human creature than a beautiful dome or steeple; and more delightful to look up reverently to a creature far above us, than to a wall; only the beautiful human creature will have some duties to do in return—duties of living belfry and rampart—of which presently.

pretending belief in a revelation which asserts the love of money to be the root of *all* evil, and declaring, at the same time, that it is actuated, and intends to be actuated, in all chief national deeds and measures, by no other love.

My friends, I do not know why any of us should talk about reading. We want some sharper discipline than that of reading; but, at all events, be assured, we cannot read. No reading is possible for a people with its mind in this state. No sentence of any great writer is intelligible to them. It is simply and sternly impossible for the English public, at this moment, to understand any thoughtful writing,—so incapable of thought has it become in its insanity of avarice. Happily, our disease is, as yet, little worse than this incapacity of thought; it is not corruption of the inner nature; we ring true still, when anything strikes home to us; and though the idea that everything should "pay" has infected our every purpose so deeply, that even when we would play the good Samaritan, we never take out our twopence and give them to the host, without saying, "When I come again, thou shalt give me fourpence," there is a capacity of noble passion left in our hearts' core. We show it in our work—in our war,—even in those unjust domestic affections which make us furious at a small private wrong, while we are polite to a boundless public one: we are still industrious to the last hour of the day, though we add the gambler's fury to the labourer's patience; we are still brave to the death, though incapable of discerning true cause for battle, and are still true in affection to our own flesh, to the death, as the sea-monsters are, and the rock-eagles. And there is hope for a nation while this can be still said of it. As long as it holds its life in its hand, ready to give it for its honour (though a foolish honour), for its love (though a selfish love), and for its business (though a base business), there is hope for it. But hope only; for this instinctive, reckless virtue cannot last. No nation can last, which has made a mob of itself, however generous at heart. It must discipline its passions, and direct them, or they will discipline it, one day, with scorpion whips. Above all, a nation cannot last as a money-making mob: it cannot with impunity,—it cannot with existence,—go on despising literature, despising science, despising art, despising nature, despising compassion, and concentrating its soul on Pence. Do you think these are harsh or wild words? Have patience with me but a little longer. I will prove their truth to you, clause by clause.

I. I say first we have despised literature. What do we, as a nation, care about books? How much do you think we spend altogether on our libraries, public or private, as compared with what we spend on our horses? If a man spends lavishly on his library, you call him mad—a biblio-maniac. But you never call any one a horse-maniac, though men ruin themselves every day by their horses, and you do not hear of people ruining themselves by their books. Or, to go lower still, how much do you think the contents of the book-shelves of the United Kingdom, public and private, would fetch, as compared with the contents of its wine-cellars? What position would its expenditure on literature take, as compared with its expenditure on luxurious eating? We talk of food for the mind, as of food for the body: now a good book contains such food inexhaustibly; it is a provision for life, and for the best part of us; yet how long most people would look at the best book before they would give the price of a large turbot for it! Though there have been men who have pinched their stomachs and bared their backs to buy a book, whose libraries were cheaper to them, I think, in the end, than most men's dinners are. We are few of us put to such trial, and more the pity; for, indeed, a precious thing is all the more precious to us if it has been won by work or economy; and if public libraries were half as costly as public dinners, or books cost the tenth part of what bracelets do, even foolish men and women might sometimes suspect there was good in reading, as well as in munching and sparkling; whereas the very cheapness of literature is making even wise people forget that if a book is worth reading, it is worth buying. No book is worth anything which is not worth *much;* nor is it serviceable, until it has been read, and reread, and loved, and loved again; and marked, so that you can refer to the passages you want in it, as a soldier can seize the weapon he needs in an armoury, or a housewife bring the spice she needs from her store. Bread of flour is good; but there is bread, sweet as honey, if we would eat it, in a good book; and the family must be poor indeed which, once in their lives, cannot, for such multipliable barley-loaves, pay their baker's bill. We call ourselves a rich nation, and we are filthy and foolish enough to thumb each other's books out of circulating libraries!

II. I say we have despised science. "What!" (you exclaim) "are we not foremost in all discovery, and is not the whole world giddy by reason, or unreason, of our inventions?" Yes; but do you suppose that is national work? That work is all done in spite of the nation; by private people's zeal and money. We are glad enough, indeed, to make our profit of science; we snap up anything in the way of a scientific bone that has meat on it, eagerly enough; but if the scientific man comes for a bone or a crust to *us*, that is another story. What have we publicly done for science? We are obliged to know what o'clock it is, for the safety of our ships, and therefore we pay for an observatory; and we allow ourselves, in the person of our Parliament, to be annually tormented into doing something, in a slovenly way, for the British Museum; sullenly apprehending that to be a place for keeping stuffed birds in, to amuse our children. If anybody will pay for their own telescope, and resolve another nebula, we cackle over the discernment as if it were our own; if one in ten thousand of our hunting squires suddenly perceives that the earth was indeed made to be something else than a portion for foxes, and burrows in it himself, and tells us where the gold is, and where the coals, we understand that there is some use in that; and very properly knight him: but is the accident of his having found out how to employ himself usefully any credit to *us?* (The negation of such discovery among his brother squires may perhaps be some *dis*credit to us, if we would consider of it.) But if you doubt these generalities, here is one fact for us all to meditate upon, illustrative of our love of science. Two years ago there was a collection of the fossils of Solenhofen to be sold in Bavaria; the best in existence, containing many specimens unique for perfectness, and one, unique as an example of a species (a whole kingdom of unknown living creatures being announced by that fossil). This collection, of which the mere market worth, among private buyers, would probably have been some thousand or twelve hundred pounds, was offered to the English nation for seven hundred: but we would not give seven hundred, and the whole series would have been in the

Munich museum at this moment, if Professor Owen* had not, with loss of his own time, and patient tormenting of the British public in person of its representatives, got leave to give four hundred pounds at once, and himself become answerable for the other three! which the said public will doubtless pay him eventually, but sulkily, and caring nothing about the matter all the while; only always ready to cackle if any credit comes of it. Consider, I beg of you, arithmetically, what this fact means. Your annual expenditure for public purposes (a third of it for military apparatus) is at least 50 millions. Now 700*l.* is to 50,000,000*l.* roughly, as seven pence to two thousand pounds. Suppose then, a gentleman of unknown income, but whose wealth was to be conjectured from the fact that he spent two thousand a year on his park-walls and footmen only, professes himself fond of science; and that one of his servants comes eagerly to tell him that an unique collection of fossils, giving clue to a new era of creation, is to be had for the sum of seven pence sterling; and that the gentleman, who is fond of science, and spends two thousand a year on his park, answers, after keeping his servant waiting several months, "Well! I'll give you four

* I state this fact without Professor Owen's permission: which of course he could not with propriety have granted, had I asked it; but I consider it so important that the public should be aware of the fact, that I do what seems to me right, though rude.

pence for them, if you will be answerable for the extra three-pence yourself, till next year!"

III. I say you have despised Art! "What!" you again answer, "have we not Art exhibitions, miles long? and do we not pay thousands of pounds for single pictures? and have we not Art schools and institutions, more than ever nation had before?" Yes, truly, but all that is for the sake of the shop. You would fain sell canvas as well as coals, and crockery as well as iron; you would take every other nation's bread out of its mouth if you could; not being able to do that, your ideal of life is to stand in the thoroughfares of the world, like Ludgate apprentices, screaming to every passer-by, "What d'ye lack?" You know nothing of your own faculties or circumstances; you fancy that, among your damp, flat, fat fields of clay, you can have as quick art-fancy as the Frenchman among his bronzed vines, or the Italian under his volcanic cliffs;—that Art may be learned as book-keeping is, and when learned, will give you more books to keep. You care for pictures, absolutely, no more than you do for the bills pasted on your dead walls. There is always room on the wall for the bills to be read,—never for the pictures to be seen. You do not know what pictures you have (by repute) in the country, nor whether they are false or true, nor whether they are taken care of or not; in foreign countries, you calmly see the noblest existing pictures in the world rotting in abandoned wreck—(and, in Venice, with the Austrian guns deliberately pointed at the palaces containing them), and if you heard that all the Titians in Europe were made sand-bags to-morrow on the Austrian forts, it would not trouble you so much as the chance of a brace or two of game less in your own bags in a day's shooting. That is your national love of Art.

IV. You have despised nature; that is to say, all the deep and sacred sensations of natural scenery. The French revolutionists made stables of the cathedrals of France; you have made racecourses of the cathedrals of the earth. Your *one* conception of pleasure is to drive in railroad carriages round their aisles, and eat off their altars. You have put a railroad bridge over the fall of Schaffhausen. You have tunnelled the cliffs of Lucerne by Tell's chapel; you have destroyed the Clarens shore of the Lake of Geneva; there is not a quiet valley in England that you have not filled with bellowing fire; there is no particle left of English land which you have not trampled coal ashes into—nor any foreign city in which the spread of your presence is not marked among its fair old streets and happy gardens by a consuming white leprosy of new hotels and perfumers' shops: the Alps themselves, which your own poets used to love so reverently, you look upon as soaped poles in a bear-garden, which you set yourselves to climb, and slide down again, with "shrieks of delight."

When you are past shrieking, having no human articulate voice to say you are glad with, you fill the quietude of their valleys with gunpowder blasts, and rush home, red with cutaneous eruption of conceit, and voluble with convulsive hiccough of self-satisfaction. I think nearly the two sorrowfullest spectacles I have ever seen in humanity, taking the deep inner significance of them, are the English mobs in the valley of Chamouni, amusing themselves with firing rusty howitzers; and the Swiss vintagers of Zurich expressing their Christian thanks for the gift of the vine, by assembling in knots in the "towers of the vineyards," and slowly loading and firing horse-pistols from morning till evening. It is pitiful to have dim conceptions of duty; more pitiful, it seems to me, to have conceptions like these, of mirth.

Lastly. You despise compassion. There is no need of words of mine for proof of this. I will merely print one of the newspaper paragraphs which I am in the habit of cutting out and throwing into my store-drawer; here is one from a *Daily Telegraph* of an early date this year; date which, though by me carelessly left unmarked, is easily discoverable; for on the back of the slip, there is the announcement that "yesterday the seventh of the special services of this year was performed by the Bishop of Ripon in St. Paul's;" and there is a pretty piece of modern political economy besides, worth preserving note of, I think, so I print it in the note below.* But my business is with the main paragraph, relating one of such facts as happen now daily, which, by chance, has taken a form in which it came before the coroner. I will print the paragraph in red.† Be sure, the facts themselves are written in that colour, in a book which we shall all of us, literate or illiterate, have to read our page of, some day.

"An inquiry was held on Friday by Mr. Richards, deputy coroner, at the White Horse Tavern, Christ Church, Spitalfields, respecting the death of Michael Collins, aged 58 years. Mary Collins, a miserable-looking woman, said that she lived with the deceased and his son in a room at 2, Cobb's court, Christ Church. Deceased was a 'translator' of boots. Witness went out and bought old boots; deceased and his son made them into good ones, and then witness sold them

* It is announced that an arrangement has been concluded between the Ministry of Finance and the Bank of Credit for the payment of the eleven millions which the State has to pay to the National Bank by the 14th inst. This sum will be raised as follows:—The eleven commercial members of the committee of the Bank of Credit will each borrow a million of florins for three months of this bank, which will accept their bills, which again will be discounted by the National Bank. By this arrangement *the National Bank will itself furnish the funds with which it will be paid.*

† The following extract was printed in *red* in the English edition.

for what she could get at the shops, which was very little indeed. Deceased and his son used to work night and day to try and get a little bread and tea, and pay for the room (2*s.* a week), so as to keep the home together. On Friday night week deceased got up from his bench and began to shiver. He threw down the boots, saying, 'Somebody else must finish them when I am gone, for I can do no more.' There was no fire, and he said, 'I would be better if I was warm.' Witness therefore took two pairs of translated boots to sell at the shop, but she could only get 14*d.* for the two pairs, for the people at the shop said, 'We must have our profit.' Witness got 14lb. of coal, and a little tea and bread. Her son sat up the whole night to make the 'translations,' to get money, but deceased died on Saturday morning. The family never had enough to eat.—Coroner: 'It seems to me deplorable that you did not go into the workhouse.'—Witness: 'We wanted the comforts of our little home.' A juror asked what the comforts were, for he only saw a little straw in the corner of the room, the windows of which were broken. The witness began to cry, and said that they had a quilt and other little things. The deceased said he never would go into the workhouse. In summer, when the season was good, they sometimes made as much as 10*s.* profit in the week. They then always saved towards the next week, which was generally a bad one. In winter they made not half so much. For three years they had been getting from bad to worse.—Cornelius Collins said that he had assisted his father since 1847. They used to work so far into the night that both nearly lost their eyesight. Witness now had a film over his eyes. Five years ago deceased applied to the parish for aid. The relieving officer gave him a 4lb. loaf, and told him if he came again he should 'get the stones.'* That disgusted

* I do not know what this means. It is curiously coincident in verbal form, with a certain passage which some of us may remember. It may perhaps be well to preserve beside this paragraph, another cutting out of my store-drawer, from the *Morning Post*, of about a parallel date, Friday, March 10th, 1865:—"The *salons* of Mme. C——, who did the honours with clever imitative grace and elegance, were crowded with princes, dukes, marquises, and counts—in fact, with the same *male* company as one meets at the parties of the Princess Metternich and Madame Drouyn de Lhuys. Some English peers and members of Parliament were present, and appeared to enjoy the animated and dazzlingly improper scene. On the second floor the supper tables were loaded with every delicacy of the season. That your readers may form some idea of the dainty fare of the Parisian demimonde, I copy the menu of the supper, which was served to all the guests (about 200) seated at four o'clock. Choice Yquem, Johannisberg, Laffitte, Tokay, and Champagne of the finest vintages were served most lavishly throughout the morning. After supper dancing was resumed with increased animation, and the ball terminated with a *chaîne diabolique* and a *cancan d'enfer* at seven in the morning. (Morning-service—'Ere the fresh lawns appeared, under the

deceased, and he would have nothing to do with them since. They got worse and worse until last Friday week, when they had not even a halfpenny to buy a candle. Deceased then lay down on the straw, and said he could not live till morning.—A juror: You are dying of starvation yourself, and you ought to go into the house until the summer. Witness: If we went in we should die. When we come out in the summer we should be like people dropped from the sky. No one would know us, and we would not have even a room. I could work now if I had food, for my sight would get better. Dr. G. P. Walker said deceased died from syncope, from exhaustion from want of food. The deceased had had no bedclothes. For four months he had had nothing but bread to eat. There was not a particle of fat in the body. There was no disease, but if there had been medical attendance, he might have survived the syncope or fainting. The coroner having remarked upon the painful nature of the case, the jury returned the following

opening eyelids of the Morn.—') Here is the menu:—'Consommé de volaille à la Bagration; 16 hors-d'œuvres variés. Bouchées à la Talleyrand. Saumons froids, sauce Ravigote. Filets de bœuf en Bellevue, timbales milanaises chaudfroid de gibier. Dindes truffées. Pâtés de foies gras, buissons d'écrevisses, salades vénétiennes, gelées blanches aux fruits, gateaux mancini, parisiens et parisiennes. Fromages glacés Ananas. Dessert.'"

verdict, 'That deceased died from exhaustion from want of food and the common necessaries of life; also through want of medical aid.'"

"Why would witness not go into the workhouse?" you ask. Well, the poor seem to have a prejudice against the workhouse which the rich have not; for of course every one who takes a pension from Government goes into the workhouse on a grand scale: only the workhouses for the rich do not involve the idea of work, and should be called play-houses. But the poor like to die independently, it appears; perhaps if we made the play-houses for them pretty and pleasant enough, or gave them their pensions at home, and allowed them a little introductory peculation with the public money, their minds might be reconciled to it. Meantime, here are the facts: we make our relief either so insulting to them, or so painful, that they rather die than take it at our hands; or, for third alternative, we leave them so untaught and foolish that they starve like brute creatures, wild and dumb, not knowing what to do, or what to ask. I say, you despise compassion; if you did not, such a newspaper paragraph would be as impossible in a Christian country as a deliberate assassination permitted in its public streets.* "Christian" did I say? Alas, if we were but

* I am heartily glad to see such a paper as the *Pall Mall Gazette*

wholesomely un-Christian, it would be impossible: it is our imaginary Christianity that helps us to commit these crimes,

established; for the power of the press in the hands of highly-educated men, in independent position, and of honest purpose, may indeed become all that it has been hitherto vainly vaunted to be. Its editor will therefore, I doubt not, pardon me, in that, by very reason of my respect for the journal, I do not let pass unnoticed an article in its third number, page 5, which was wrong in every word of it, with the intense wrongness which only an honest man can achieve who has taken a false turn of thought in the outset, and is following it, regardless of consequences. It contained at the end this notable passage:—

"The bread of affliction, and the water of affliction—aye, and the bedsteads and blankets of affliction, are the very utmost that the law ought to give to *outcasts merely as outcasts.*" I merely put beside this expression of the gentlemanly mind of England in 1865, a part of the message which Isaiah was ordered to "lift up his voice like a trumpet" in declaring to the gentlemen of his day: "Ye fast for strife, and to smite with the fist of wickedness. Is not this the fast that I have chosen, to deal thy bread to the hungry, and that thou bring the poor *that are cast out* (margin 'afflicted') to *thy* house." The falsehood on which the writer had mentally founded himself, as previously stated by him, was this: "To confound the functions of the dispensers of the poor-rates with those of the dispensers of a charitable institution is a great and pernicious error." This sentence is so accurately and exquisitely wrong, that its substance must be thus reversed in our minds before we can deal with any existing problem of national distress. "To understand that the dispensers of the poor-rates are the almoners of the nation, and should distribute its alms with a for we revel and luxuriate in our faith, for the lewd sensation of it; dressing *it* up, like everything else, in fiction. The dramatic Christianity of the organ and aisle, of dawn-service and twilight-revival—the Christianity which we do not fear to mix the mockery of, pictorially, with our play about the devil, in our Satanellas,—Roberts,—Fausts, chanting hymns through traceried windows for back-ground effect, and artistically modulating the "Dio" through variation on variation of mimicked prayer: (while we distribute tracts, next day, for the benefit of uncultivated swearers, upon what we suppose to be the signification of the Third Commandment;)—this gas-lighted, and gas-inspired, Christianity, we are triumphant in, and draw back the hem of our robes from the touch of the heretics who dispute it. But to do a piece of common Christian righteousness in a plain English word or deed; to make Christian law any rule of life, and found one National act or hope thereon,—we know too well what our faith comes to for that! You might sooner get lightning out of incense smoke than true action or passion out of your modern English religion. You had better get rid of the smoke, and the organ pipes, both: leave them, and the

gentleness and freedom of hand as much greater and franker than that possible to individual charity, as the collective national wisdom and power may be supposed greater than those of any single person, is the foundation of all law respecting pauperism."

Gothic windows, and the painted glass, to the property man; give up your carburetted hydrogen ghost in one healthy expiration, and look after Lazarus at the door-step. For there is a true Church wherever one hand meets another helpfully, and that is the only holy or Mother Church which ever was, or ever shall be.

All these pleasures, then, and all these virtues, I repeat, you nationally despise. You have, indeed, men among you who do not; by whose work, by whose strength, by whose life, by whose death, you live, and never thank them. Your wealth, your amusement, your pride, would all be alike impossible, but for those whom you scorn or forget. The policeman, who is walking up and down the black lane all night to watch the guilt you have created there, and may have his brains beaten out and be maimed for life at any moment, and never be thanked; the sailor wrestling with the sea's rage; the quiet student poring over his book or his vial; the common worker, without praise, and nearly without bread, fulfilling his task as your horses drag your carts, hopeless, and spurned of all: these are the men by whom England lives; but they are not the nation; they are only the body and nervous force of it, acting still from old habit in a convulsive perseverance, while the mind is gone. Our National mind and purpose are to be amused; our National religion, the performance of church ceremonies, and preaching of soporific truths (or untruths) to keep the mob quietly at work, while we amuse ourselves; and the necessity for this amusement is fastening on us as a feverous disease of parched throat and wandering eyes — senseless, dissolute, merciless. When men are rightly occupied, their amusement grows out of their work, as the colour-petals out of a fruitful flower;—when they are faithfully helpful and compassionate, all their emotions become steady, deep, perpetual, and vivifying to the soul as the natural pulse to the body. But now, having no true business, we pour our whole masculine energy into the false business of money-making; and having no true emotion, we must have false emotions dressed up for us to play with, not innocently, as children with dolls, but guiltily and darkly, as the idolatrous Jews with their pictures on cavern walls, which men had to dig to detect. The justice we do not execute, we mimic in the novel and on the stage; for the beauty we destroy in nature, we substitute the metamorphosis of the pantomime, and (the human nature of us imperatively requiring awe and sorrow of *some* kind) for the noble grief we should have borne with our fellows, and the pure tears we should have wept with them, we gloat over the pathos of the police court, and gather the night-dew of the grave.

It is difficult to estimate the true significance of these things; the facts are frightful enough;—the measure of national fault involved in them is perhaps not as great as it would at first seem. We permit, or cause, thousands of deaths daily, but we mean no harm; we set fire to houses, and ravage peasants' fields; yet we should be sorry to find we had injured anybody. We are still kind at heart; still capable of virtue, but only as children are. Chalmers, at the end of his long life, having had much power with the public, being plagued in some serious matter by a reference to "public opinion," uttered the impatient exclamation, "The public is just a great baby!" And the reason that I have allowed all these graver subjects of thought to mix themselves up with an inquiry into methods of reading, is that, the more I see of our national faults or miseries, the more they resolve themselves into conditions of childish illiterateness, and want of education in the most ordinary habits of thought. It is, I repeat, not vice, not selfishness, not dulness of brain, which we have to lament; but an unreachable schoolboy's recklessness, only differing from the true schoolboy's in its incapacity of being helped, because it acknowledges no master. There is a curious type of us given in one of the lovely, neglected works of the last of our great painters. It is a drawing of Kirkby Lonsdale churchyard, and of its brook, and valley, and hills, and folded morning sky beyond. And unmindful alike of these, and of the dead who have left these for other valleys and for other skies, a group of schoolboys have piled their little books upon a grave, to strike them off with stones. So do we play with the words of the dead that would teach us, and strike them far from us with our bitter, reckless will, little thinking that those leaves which the wind scatters had been piled, not only upon a gravestone, but upon the seal of an enchanted vault—nay, the gate of a great city of sleeping kings, who would awake for us, and walk with us, if we knew but how to call them by their names. How often, even if we lift the marble entrance gate, do we but wander among those old kings in their repose, and finger the robes they lie in, and stir the crowns on their foreheads; and still they are silent to us, and seem but a dusty imagery; because we know not the incantation of the heart that would wake them;—which, if they once heard, they would start up to meet us in their power of long ago, narrowly to look upon us, and consider us; and, as the fallen kings of Hades meet the newly fallen, saying, "Art thou also become weak as we—art thou also become one of us?" so would these kings, with their undimmed, unshaken diadems, meet us, saying, "Art thou also become pure and mighty of heart as we? art thou also become one of us?"

Mighty of heart, mighty of mind—"magnanimous"—to be this, is indeed to be great in life; to become this increasingly, is, indeed, to "advance in life,"—in life itself—not in the trappings of it. My friends, do you remember that old Scythian custom, when the head of a house died? How he was dressed in his finest dress, and set in his chariot, and carried about to his friends' houses; and each of them placed him at his table's head, and all feasted in his presence? Suppose it were offered to you, in plain words, as it *is* offered to you in dire facts, that you should gain this Scythian honour, gradually, while you yet thought yourself alive. Suppose the offer were this: "You shall die slowly; your blood shall daily grow cold, your flesh petrify, your heart beat at last only as a rusted group of iron valves. Your life shall fade from you, and sink through the earth into the ice of Caina; but, day by day, your body shall be dressed more gaily, and set in higher chariots, and have more orders on its breast—crowns on its head, if you will. Men shall bow before it, stare and shout round it, crowd after it up and down the streets; build palaces for it, feast with it at their tables' heads all the night long; your soul shall stay enough within it to know what they do, and feel the weight of the golden dress on its shoulders, and the furrow of the crown-edge on the skull;—no more. Would you take the offer, verbally made by the death-angel? Would the meanest among us take it, think you? Yet practically and verily we grasp at it, every one of us, in a measure; many of us grasp at it in its fulness of horror. Every man accepts it, who desires to advance in life without knowing what life is; who means only that he is to get more horses, and more footmen, and more fortune, and more public honour, and—*not* more personal soul. He only is advancing in life, whose heart is getting softer, whose blood warmer, whose brain quicker, whose spirit is entering into Living* peace. And the men who have this life in them are the true lords or kings of the earth—they, and they only. All other kingships, so far as they are true, are only the practical issue and expression of theirs; if less than this, they are either dramatic royalties,—costly shows, with real jewels instead of tinsel—the toys of nations; or else, they are no royalties at all, but tyrannies, or the mere active and practical issue of national folly; for which reason I have said of them elsewhere, "Visible governments are the toys of some nations, the diseases of others, the harness of some, the burdens of more."

But I have no words for the wonder with which I hear Kinghood still spoken of, even among thoughtful men, as if governed nations were a personal property, and might be bought and sold, or otherwise acquired, as sheep, of whose flesh their king was to feed, and whose fleece he was to gather; as if Achilles' indignant epithet of base kings, "people-eating," were the constant and proper title of all monarchs; and enlargement of a king's dominion meant the

* "τὸ δὲ φρόνημα τοῦ πνεύματος ζωὴ καὶ εἰρήνη."

same thing as the increase of a private man's estate! Kings who think so, however powerful, can no more be the true kings of the nation than gad-flies are the kings of a horse; they suck it, and may drive it wild, but do not guide it. They, and their courts, and their armies are, if one could see clearly, only a large species of marsh mosquito, with bayonet proboscis and melodious, band-mastered, trumpeting in the summer air; the twilight being, perhaps, sometimes fairer, but hardly more wholesome, for its glittering mists of midge companies. The true kings, meanwhile, rule quietly, if at all, and hate ruling; too many of them make "il gran refiúto;" and if they do not, the mob, as soon as they are likely to become useful to it, is pretty sure to make *its* "gran refiúto" of *them.*

Yet the visible king may also be a true one, some day, if ever day comes when he will estimate his dominion by the *force* of it,—not the geographical boundaries. It matters very little whether Trent cuts you a cantel out here, or Rhine rounds you a castle less there. But it does matter to you, king of men, whether you can verily say to this man, "Go," and he goeth; and to another, "Come," and he cometh. Whether you can turn your people as you can Trent—and where it is that you bid them come, and where go. It matters to you, king of men, whether your people hate you, and die by you, or love you, and live by you.

You may measure your dominion by multitudes better than by miles; and count degrees of love-latitude, not from, but to, a wonderfully warm and infinite equator. Measure! nay you cannot measure. Who shall measure the difference between the power of those who "do and teach," and who are greatest in the kingdoms of earth, as of heaven—and the power of those who undo, and consume—whose power, at the fullest, is only the power of the moth and the rust? Strange! to think how the Moth-kings lay up treasures for the moth, and the Rust-kings, who are to their peoples' strength as rust to armour, lay up treasures for the rust; and the Robber-kings, treasures for the robber; but how few kings have ever laid up treasures that needed no guarding—treasures of which, the more thieves there were, the better! Broidered robe, only to be rent—helm and sword, only to be dimmed; jewel and gold, only to be scattered—there have been three kinds of kings who have gathered these. Suppose there ever should arise a Fourth order of kings, who had read, in some obscure writing of long ago, that there was a Fourth kind of treasure, which the jewel and gold could not equal, neither should it be valued with pure gold. A web more fair in the weaving, by Athena's shuttle; an armour, forged in diviner fire by Vulcanian force—a gold only to be mined in the sun's red heart, where he sets over the Delphian cliffs;—deep-pictured tissue, impenetrable armour, potable gold!—the three great Angels of Conduct, Toil, and Thought, still calling to us, and waiting at the posts of our doors, to lead us, if we would, with their winged power, and guide us, with their inescapable eyes, by the path which no fowl knoweth, and which the vulture's eye has not seen! Suppose kings should ever arise, who heard and believed this word, and at last gathered and brought forth treasures of—Wisdom—for their people?

Think what an amazing business *that* would be! How inconceivable, in the state of our present national wisdom. That we should bring up our peasants to a book exercise instead of a bayonet exercise!—organize, drill, maintain with pay, and good generalship, armies of thinkers, instead of armies of stabbers!—find national amusement in reading-rooms as well as rifle-grounds; give prizes for a fair shot at a fact, as well as for a leaden splash on a target. What an absurd idea it seems, put fairly in words, that the wealth of the capitalists of civilized nations should ever come to support literature instead of war! Have yet patience with me, while I read you a single sentence out of the only book, properly to be called a book, that I have yet written myself, the one that will stand, (if anything stand,) surest and longest of all work of mine.

"It is one very awful form of the operation of wealth in Europe that it is entirely capitalists' wealth which supports unjust wars. Just wars do not need so much money to support them; for most of the men who wage such, wage them gratis; but for an unjust war, men's bodies and souls have both to be bought; and the best tools of war for them besides, which makes such war costly to the maximum; not to speak of the cost of base fear, and angry suspicion, between nations which have not grace nor honesty enough in all their multitudes to buy an hour's peace of mind with; as, at present France and England, purchasing of each other ten millions' sterling worth of consternation, annually (a remarkably light crop, half thorns and half aspen leaves, sown, reaped, and granaried by the 'science' of the modern political economist, teaching covetousness instead of truth). And, all unjust war being supportable, if not by pillage of the enemy, only by loans from capitalists, these loans are repaid by subsequent taxation of the people, who appear to have no will in the matter, the capitalists' will being the primary root of the war; but its real root is the covetousness of the whole nation, rendering it incapable of faith, frankness, or justice, and bringing about, therefore, in due time, his own separate loss and punishment to each person."

France and England literally, observe, buy *panic* of each other; they pay, each of them, for ten thousand thousand pounds' worth of terror, a year. Now suppose, instead of buying these ten millions' worth of panic annually, they made up their minds to be at peace with each other, and buy ten millions' worth of knowledge annually; and that each nation spent its ten thousand thousand pounds a year in founding royal libraries, royal art galleries, royal museums, royal gardens, and places of rest. Might it not be better somewhat for both French and English?

It will be long, yet, before that comes to pass. Nevertheless, I hope it will not be long before royal or national libraries will be founded in every considerable city, with a royal series of books in them; the same series in every one of them, chosen books, the best in every kind, prepared for that national series in the most perfect way possible; their text printed all on leaves of equal size, broad of margin, and divided into pleasant volumes, light in the hand, beautiful, and strong, and thorough as examples of binders' work; and that these great libraries will be accessible to all clean and orderly persons at all times of the day and evening; strict law being enforced for this cleanliness and quietness.

I could shape for you other plans, for art-galleries, and for natural history galleries, and for many precious, many, it seems to me, needful, things; but this book plan is the easiest and needfullest, and would prove a considerable tonic to what we call our British constitution, which has fallen dropsical of late, and has an evil thirst, and evil hunger, and wants healthier feeding. You have got its corn laws repealed for it; try if you cannot get corn laws established for it, dealing in a better bread;—bread made of that old enchanted Arabian grain, the Sesame, which opens doors;—doors, not of robbers', but of Kings' Treasuries.

Friends, the treasuries of true kings are the streets of their cities; and the gold they gather, which for others is as the mire of the streets, changes itself, for them and their people, into a crystalline pavement for evermore.

LECTURE II.—LILIES.

OF QUEENS' GARDENS.

"ὡς κρίνον ἐν μέσῳ ἀκανθῶν, οὕτως ἡ πλησίον μου."*

It will, perhaps, be well, as this Lecture is the sequel of one previously given, that I should shortly state to you my general intention in both. The questions specially proposed to you in the first, namely, How and What to Read, rose out of a far deeper one, which it was my endeavour to make you propose earnestly to yourselves, namely, *Why* to Read. I want you to feel, with me, that whatever advantages we possess in the present day in the diffusion of education and of literature, can only be rightly used by any of us when we have apprehended clearly what education is to lead to, and literature to teach. I wish you to see that both well-directed moral training and well-chosen reading lead to the possession of a power over the ill-guided and illiterate, which is, according to the measure of it, in the truest sense, *kingly;* conferring indeed the purest kingship that can exist among men: too many other kingships (however distinguished by visible insignia or material power) being either spectral, or tyrannous;—

* Canticles ii. 2.

Spectral—that is to say, aspects and shadows only of royalty, hollow as death, and which only the "Likeness of a kingly crown have on;" or else tyrannous—that is to say, substituting their own will for the law of justice and love by which all true kings rule.

There is, then, I repeat—and as I want to leave this idea with you, I begin with it, and shall end with it—only one pure kind of kingship; an inevitable and eternal kind, crowned or not: the kingship, namely, which consists in a stronger moral state, and a truer thoughtful state, than that of others; enabling you, therefore, to guide, or to raise them. Observe that word "State;" we have got into a loose way of using it. It means literally the standing and stability of a thing; and you have the full force of it in the derived word "statue"—"the immoveable thing." A king's majesty or "state," then, and the right of his kingdom to be called a state, depends on the movelessness of both:—without tremor, without quiver of balance; established and enthroned upon a foundation of eternal law which nothing can alter nor overthrow.

Believing that all literature and all education are only useful so far as they tend to confirm this calm, beneficent, and *therefore* kingly, power—first, over ourselves, and, through ourselves, over all around us, I am now going to ask you to consider with me farther, what special portion or kind of this royal authority, arising out of noble education, may rightly be possessed by women; and how far they also are called to a true queenly power. Not in their households merely, but over all within their sphere. And in what sense, if they rightly understood and exercised this royal or gracious influence, the order and beauty induced by such benignant power would justify us in speaking of the territories over which each of them reigned, as "Queens' Gardens."

And here, in the very outset, we are met by a far deeper question, which—strange though this may seem—remains among many of us yet quite undecided, in spite of its infinite importance.

We cannot determine what the queenly power of women should be, until we are agreed what their ordinary power should be. We cannot consider how education may fit them for any widely extending duty, until we are agreed what is their true constant duty. And there never was a time when wilder words were spoken, or more vain imagination permitted, respecting this question—quite vital to all social happiness. The relations of the womanly to the manly nature, their different capacities of intellect or of virtue, seem never to have been yet measured with entire consent. We hear of the mission and of the rights of Woman, as if these could ever be separate from the mission and the rights of Man;—as if she and her lord were creatures of independent kind and of irreconcileable claim. This, at least, is wrong. And not less wrong—perhaps even more foolishly wrong (for I will anticipate thus far what I hope to prove)—is the idea that woman is only the shadow and attendant image of her lord, owing him a thoughtless and servile obedience, and supported altogether in her weakness by the pre-eminence of his fortitude.

This, I say, is the most foolish of all errors respecting her who was made to be the helpmate of man. As if he could be helped effectively by a shadow, or worthily by a slave!

Let us try, then, whether we cannot get at some clear and harmonious idea (it must be harmonious if it is true) of what womanly mind and virtue are in power and office, with respect to man's; and how their relations, rightly accepted, aid, and increase, the vigour, and honour, and authority of both.

And now I must repeat one thing I said in the last lecture: namely, that the first use of education was to enable us to consult with the wisest and the greatest men on all points of earnest difficulty. That to use books rightly, was to go to them for help: to appeal to them, when our own knowledge and power of thought failed; to be led by them into wider sight, purer conception than our own, and receive from them the united sentence of the judges and councils of all time, against our solitary and unstable opinion.

Let us do this now. Let us see whether the greatest, the wisest, the purest-hearted of all ages are agreed in any wise on this point: let us hear the testimony they have left respecting what they held to be the true dignity of woman, and her mode of help to man.

And first let us take Shakespeare.

Note broadly in the outset, Shakespeare has no heroes;—he has only heroines. There is not one entirely heroic figure in all his plays, except the slight sketch of Henry the Fifth, exaggerated for the purposes of the stage; and the still slighter Valentine in The Two Gentlemen of Verona. In his laboured and perfect plays you have no hero. Othello would have been one, if his simplicity had not been so great as to leave him the prey of every base practice round him; but he is the only example even approximating to the heroic type. Coriolanus—Cæsar—Antony, stand in flawed strength, and fall by their vanities;—Hamlet is indolent, and drowsily speculative; Romeo an impatient boy; the Merchant of Venice languidly submissive to adverse fortune; Kent, in King Lear, is entirely noble at heart, but too rough and unpolished to be of true use at the critical time, and he sinks into the office of a servant only. Orlando, no less noble, is yet the despairing toy of chance, followed, comforted, saved, by Rosalind. Whereas there is hardly a play that has not a perfect woman in it, steadfast in grave hope, and errorless purpose; Cordelia, Desdemona, Isabella, Hermione, Imogen, Queen Katherine, Perdita, Sylvia, Viola, Rosalind, Helena, and last, and perhaps loveliest, Virgilia, are all faultless; conceived in the highest heroic type of humanity.

Then observe, secondly,

The catastrophe of every play is caused always by the folly or fault of a man; the redemption, if there be any, is by the wisdom and virtue of a woman, and, failing that, there is none. The catastrophe of King Lear is owing to his own want of judgment, his impatient vanity, his misunderstanding of his children; the virtue of his one true daughter would have saved him from all the injuries of the others, unless he had cast her away from him; as it is, she all but saves him.

Of Othello I need not trace the tale;—nor the one weakness of his so mighty love; nor the inferiority of his perceptive intellect to that even of the second woman character in the play, the Emilia who dies in wild testimony against his error:—"Oh, murderous coxcomb! What should such a fool Do with so good a wife?"

In Romeo and Juliet, the wise and entirely brave stratagem of the wife is brought to ruinous issue by the reckless impatience of her husband. In Winter's Tale, and in Cymbeline, the happiness and existence of two princely households, lost through long years, and imperilled to the death by the folly and obstinacy of the husbands, are redeemed at last by the queenly patience and wisdom of the wives. In Measure for Measure, the injustice of the judges, and the corrupt cowardice of the brother, are opposed to the victorious truth and adamantine purity of a woman. In Coriolanus, the mother's counsel, acted upon in time, would have saved her son from all evil; his momentary forgetfulness of it is his ruin; her prayer at last granted, saves him—not, indeed, from death, but from the curse of living as the destroyer of his country.

And what shall I say of Julia, constant against the fickleness of a lover who is a mere wicked child?—of Helena, against the petulance and insult of a careless youth?—of the patience of Hero, the passion of Beatrice, and the calmly devoted wisdom of the "unlessoned girl," who appears among the helplessness, the blindness, and the vindictive passions of men, as a gentle angel, to save merely by her presence, and defeat the worst intensities of crime by her smile?

Observe, further, among all the principal figures in Shakespeare's plays, there is only one weak woman—Ophelia; and it is because she fails Hamlet at the critical moment, and is not, and cannot in her nature be, a guide to him when he needs her most, that all the bitter catastrophe follows. Finally, though there are three wicked women among the principal figures, Lady Macbeth, Regan, and Goneril, they are felt at once to be frightful exceptions to the ordinary laws of life; fatal in their influence also in proportion to the power for good which they have abandoned.

Such, in broad light, is Shakespeare's testimony to the position and character of women in human life. He represents them as infallibly faithful and wise counsellors,—incorruptibly just and pure examples—strong always to sanctify, even when they cannot save.

Not as in any wise comparable in knowledge of the nature of man,—still less in his understanding of the causes and courses of fate,—but only as the writer who has given us the broadest view of the conditions and modes of ordinary thought in modern society, I ask you next to receive the witness of Walter Scott.

I put aside his merely romantic prose writings as of no value: and though the early romantic poetry is very beautiful, its testimony is of no weight, other than that of a boy's ideal. But his true works, studied from Scottish life, bear a true witness, and in the whole range of these there are but three men who reach the heroic type—Dandie Dinmont, Rob Roy, and Claverhouse: of these, one is a border farmer; another a freebooter; the third a soldier in a bad cause. And these touch the ideal of heroism only in their courage and faith, together with a strong, but uncultivated, or mistakenly applied, intellectual power; while his younger men are the gentlemanly playthings of fantastic fortune, and only by aid (or accident) of that fortune, survive, not vanquish, the trials they involuntarily sustain. Of any disciplined, or consistent character, earnest in a purpose wisely conceived, or dealing with forms of hostile evil, definitely challenged, and resolutely subdued, there is no trace in his conceptions of men. Whereas in his imaginations of women,—in the characters of Ellen Douglas, of Flora MacIvor, Rose Bradwardine, Catherine Seyton, Diana Vernon, Lilias Redgauntlet, Alice Bridgenorth, Alice Lee, and Jeanie Deans,—with endless varieties of grace, tenderness, and intellectual power, we find in all a quite infallible and inevitable sense of dignity and justice; a fearless, instant, and untiring self-sacrifice to even the appearance of duty, much more to its real claims; and, finally, a patient wisdom of deeply restrained affection, which does infinitely more than protect its objects from a momentary error; it gradually forms, animates, and exalts the characters of the unworthy lovers, until, at the close of the tale, we are just able, and no more, to take patience in hearing of their unmerited success.

So that in all cases, with Scott as with Shakespeare, it is the woman who watches over, teaches, and guides the youth; it is never, by any chance, the youth who watches over or educates his mistress.

Next, take, though more briefly, graver and deeper testimony—that of the great Italians and Greeks. You know well the plan of Dante's great poem—that it is a love-poem to his dead lady, a song of praise for her watch over his soul. Stooping only to pity, never to love, she yet saves him from destruction—saves him from hell. He is going eternally astray in despair; she comes down from heaven to his help, and throughout the ascents of Paradise is his teacher, interpreting for him the most difficult truths, divine and human; and leading him, with rebuke upon rebuke, from star to star.

I do not insist upon Dante's conception; if I began I could not cease: besides, you might think this a wild imagination of one poet's heart. So I will rather read to you a few verses of the deliberate writing of a knight of Pisa to his living lady, wholly characteristic of the feeling of all the noblest men of the thirteenth century, preserved among many other such records of knightly honour and love, which Dante Rossetti has gathered for us from among the early Italian poets.

For lo! thy law is passed
That this my love should manifestly be
To serve and honour thee:
And so I do; and my delight is full,
Accepted for the servant of thy rule.

Without almost, I am all rapturous,
Since thus my will was set

To serve, thou flower of joy, thine excellence:
Nor ever seems it anything could rouse
A pain or regret,
But on thee dwells mine every thought and sense:
Considering that from thee all virtues spread
As from a fountain head,—
That in thy gift is wisdom's best avail,
And honour without fail;
With whom each sovereign good dwells separate,
Fulfilling the perfection of thy state.

Lady, since I conceived
Thy pleasurable aspect in my heart,
My life has been apart
In shining brightness and the place of truth;
Which till that time, good sooth,
Groped among shadows in a darken'd place,
Where many hours and days
It hardly ever had remember'd good.
But now my servitude
Is thine, and I am full of joy and rest.
A man from a wild beast
Thou madest me, since for thy love I lived.

You may think, perhaps, a Greek knight would have had a lower estimate of women than this Christian lover. His own spiritual subjection to them was indeed not so absolute;

but as regards their own personal character, it was only because you could not have followed me so easily, that I did not take the Greek women instead of Shakespeare's; and instance, for chief ideal types of human beauty and faith, the simple mother's and wife's heart of Andromache; the divine, yet rejected wisdom of Cassandra; the playful kindness and simple princess-life of happy Nausicaa; the housewifely calm of that of Penelope, with its watch upon the sea; the ever patient, fearless, hopelessly devoted piety of the sister, and daughter, in Antigone; the bowing down of Iphigenia, lamb-like and silent; and, finally, the expectation of the resurrection, made clear to the soul of the Greeks in the return from her grave of that Alcestis, who, to save her husband, had passed calmly through the bitterness of death.

Now I could multiply witness upon witness of this kind upon you if I had time. I would take Chaucer, and show you why he wrote a Legend of Good Women; but no Legend of Good Men. I would take Spenser, and show you how all his fairy knights are sometimes deceived and sometimes vanquished; but the soul of Una is never darkened, and the spear of Britomart is never broken. Nay, I could go back into the mythical teaching of the most ancient times, and show you how the great people,—by one of whose princesses it was appointed that the Lawgiver of all the earth should be educated, rather than by his own kindred;—how that great Egyptian people, wisest then of nations, gave to their Spirit of Wisdom the form of a woman; and into her hand, for a symbol, the weaver's shuttle: and how the name and the form of that spirit, adopted, believed, and obeyed by the Greeks, became that Athena of the olive-helm, and cloudy shield, to whose faith you owe, down to this date, whatever you hold most precious in art, in literature, or in types of national virtue.

But I will not wander into this distant and mythical element; I will only ask you to give its legitimate value to the testimony of these great poets and men of the world,—consistent as you see it is on this head. I will ask you whether it can be supposed that these men, in the main work of their lives, are amusing themselves with a fictitious and idle view of the relations between man and woman;—nay, worse than fictitious or idle; for a thing may be imaginary, yet desirable, if it were possible; but this, their ideal of women, is, according to our common idea of the marriage relation, wholly undesirable. The woman, we say, is not to guide, nor even to think, for herself. The man is always to be the wiser; he is to be the thinker, the ruler, the superior in knowledge and discretion, as in power. Is it not somewhat important to make up our minds on this matter? Are all these great men mistaken, or are we? Are Shakespeare and Æschylus, Dante and Homer, merely dressing dolls for us; or, worse than dolls, unnatural visions, the realization of which, were it possible, would bring anarchy into all households and ruin into all affections? Nay, if you could suppose this, take lastly the evidence of facts, given by the human heart itself. In all Christian ages which have been remarkable for their purity or progress, there has been absolute yielding of obedient devotion, by the lover, to his mistress. I say *obedient*—not merely enthusiastic and worshipping in imagination, but entirely subject, receiving from the beloved woman, however young, not only the encouragement, the praise, and the reward of all toil, but, so far as any choice is open, or any question difficult of decision, the *direction* of all toil. That chivalry, to the abuse and dishonour of which are attributable primarily whatever is cruel in war, unjust in peace, or corrupt and ignoble in domestic relations; and to the original purity and power of which we owe the defence alike of faith, of law, and of love;—that chivalry, I say, in its very first conception of honourable life, assumes the subjection of the young knight to the command—should it even be the command in caprice—of his lady. It assumes this, because its masters knew that the first and necessary impulse of every truly taught and knightly heart is this of blind service to its lady: that where that true faith and captivity are not, all wayward and wicked passion must be; and that in this rapturous obedience to the single love of his youth, is the sanctification of all man's strength, and the continuance of all his purposes. And this, not because such obedience would be safe, or honourable, were it ever rendered to the unworthy; but because it ought to be impossible for every noble youth—it *is* impossible for every one rightly trained—to love any one whose gentle counsel he cannot trust, or whose prayerful command he can hesitate to obey.

I do not insist by any farther argument on this, for I think it should commend itself at once to your knowledge of what has been and to your feeling of what should be. You cannot think that the buckling on of the knight's armour by his lady's hand was a mere caprice of romantic fashion. It is the type of an eternal truth—that the soul's armour is never well set to the heart unless a woman's hand has braced it; and it is only when she braces it loosely that the honour of manhood fails. Know you not those lovely lines—I would they were learned by all youthful ladies of England:—

"Ah wasteful woman! she who may
On her sweet self set her own price,
Knowing he cannot choose but pay—

How has she cheapen'd Paradise!
How given for nought her priceless gift,
How spoiled the bread and spill'd the wine,
Which, spent with due, respective thrift,
Had made brutes men, and men divine!" *

Thus much, then, respecting the relations of lovers I believe you will accept. But what we too often doubt is the fitness of the continuance of such a relation throughout the whole of human life. We think it right in the lover and mistress, not in the husband and wife. That is to say, we think that a reverent and tender duty is due to one whose affection we still doubt, and whose character we as yet do but partially and distantly discern; and that this reverence and duty are to be withdrawn when the affection has become wholly and limitlessly our own, and the character has been so sifted and tried that we fear not to entrust it with the happiness of our lives. Do you not see how ignoble this is, as well as how unreasonable? Do you not feel that marriage—when it is marriage at all,—is only the seal which marks the vowed transition of temporary into untiring service, and of fitful into eternal love?

But how, you will ask, is the idea of this guiding function of the woman reconcileable with a true wifely subjection? Simply in that it is a *guiding*, not a determining, function.

* Coventry Patmore.

Let me try to show you briefly how these powers seem to be rightly distinguishable.

We are foolish, and without excuse foolish, in speaking of the "superiority" of one sex to the other, as if they could be compared in similar things. Each has what the other has not: each completes the other, and is completed by the other: they are in nothing alike, and the happiness and perfection of both depends on each asking and receiving from the other what the other only can give.

Now their separate characters are briefly these. The man's power is active, progressive, defensive. He is eminently the doer, the creator, the discoverer, the defender. His intellect is for speculation and invention; his energy for adventure, for war, and for conquest, wherever war is just, wherever conquest necessary. But the woman's power is for rule, not for battle,—and her intellect is not for invention or creation, but for sweet ordering, arrangement, and decision. She sees the qualities of things, their claims and their places. Her great function is Praise: she enters into no contest, but infallibly judges the crown of contest. By her office, and place, she is protected from all danger and temptation. The man, in his rough work in open world, must encounter all peril and trial:—to him, therefore, the failure, the offence, the inevitable error: often he must be wounded, or subdued, often misled, and *always* hardened. But he guards the woman from all this; within his house, as ruled by her, unless she herself has sought it, need enter no danger, no temptation, no cause of error or offence. This is the true nature of home—it is the place of Peace; the shelter, not only from all injury, but from all terror, doubt, and division. In so far as it is not this, it is not home; so far as the anxieties of the outer life penetrate into it, and the inconsistently-minded, unknown, unloved, or hostile society of the outer world is allowed by either husband or wife to cross the threshold, it ceases to be home; it is then only a part of that outer world which you have roofed over, and lighted fire in. But so far as it is a sacred place, a vestal temple, a temple of the hearth watched over by Household Gods, before whose faces none may come but those whom they can receive with love,—so far as it is this, and roof and fire are types only of a nobler shade and light,—shade as of the rock in a weary land, and light as of the Pharos in the stormy sea;—so far it vindicates the name, and fulfils the praise, of home.

And wherever a true wife comes, this home is always round her. The stars only may be over her head; the glow-worm in the night-cold grass may be the only fire at her foot: but home is yet wherever she is; and for a noble woman it stretches far round her, better than ceiled with cedar, or painted with vermilion, shedding its quiet light far, for those who else were homeless.

This, then, I believe to be,—will you not admit it to be,—the woman's true place and power? But do not you see that to fulfil this, she must—as far as one can use such terms of a human creature—be incapable of error? So far as she rules, all must be right, or nothing is. She must be enduringly, incorruptibly good; instinctively, infallibly wise—wise, not for self-development, but for self-renunciation: wise, not that she may set herself above her husband, but that she may never fail from his side: wise, not with the narrowness of insolent and loveless pride, but with the passionate gentleness of an infinitely variable, because infinitely applicable, modesty of service—the true changefulness of woman. In that great sense—"La donna e mobile," not "Qual piŭm' al vento;" no, nor yet "Variable as the shade, by the light quivering aspen made;" but variable as the *light*, manifold in fair and serene division, that it may take the colour of all that it falls upon, and exalt it.

II. I have been trying, thus far, to show you what should be the place, and what the power of woman. Now, secondly, we ask, What kind of education is to fit her for these?

And if you indeed think this a true conception of her office and dignity, it will not be difficult to trace the course of education which would fit her for the one, and raise her to the other.

The first of our duties to her—no thoughtful persons now

doubt this,—is to secure for her such physical training and exercise as may confirm her health, and perfect her beauty: the highest refinement of that beauty being unattainable without splendour of activity and of delicate strength. To perfect her beauty, I say, and increase its power; it cannot be too powerful, nor shed its sacred light too far: only remember that all physical freedom is vain to produce beauty without a corresponding freedom of heart. There are two passages of that poet who is distinguished, it seems to me, from all others—not by power, but by exquisite *right*ness—which point you to the source, and describe to you, in a few syllables, the completion of womanly beauty. I will read the introductory stanzas, but the last is the one I wish you specially to notice:

> "Three years she grew in sun and shower,
> Then Nature said, a lovelier flower
>   On earth was never sown.
> This child I to myself will take;
> She shall be mine, and I will make
>   A lady of my own.
>
> "Myself will to my darling be
> Both law and impulse; and with me
>   The girl, in rock and plain,
> In earth and heaven, in glade and bower,

Shall feel an overseeing power
To kindle, or restrain.

"The floating clouds their state shall lend
To her, for her the willow bend;
Nor shall she fail to see
Even in the motions of the storm,
Grace that shall mould the maiden's form
By silent sympathy.

"And *vital feelings of delight*
Shall rear her form to stately height,—
Her virgin bosom swell.
Such *thoughts* to Lucy I will give,
While she and I together live,
Here in this happy dell."

"*Vital* feelings of delight," observe. There are deadly feelings of delight; but the natural ones are vital, necessary to very life.

And they must be feelings of delight, if they are to be vital. Do not think you can make a girl lovely, if you do not make her happy. There is not one restraint you put on a good girl's nature—there is not one check you give to her instincts of affection or of effort—which will not be indelibly written on her features, with a hardness which is all the more painful because it takes away the brightness from the eyes of innocence, and the charm from the brow of virtue.

This for the means: now note the end. Take from the same poet, in two lines, a perfect description of womanly beauty—

> "A countenance in which did meet
> Sweet records, promises as sweet."

The perfect loveliness of a woman's countenance can only consist in that majestic peace, which is founded in the memory of happy and useful years,—full of sweet records; and from the joining of this with that yet more majestic childishness, which is still full of change and promise;—opening always—modest at once, and bright, with hope of better things to be won, and to be bestowed. There is no old age where there is still that promise—it is eternal youth.

Thus, then, you have first to mould her physical frame, and then, as the strength she gains will permit you, to fill and temper her mind with all knowledge and thoughts which tend to confirm its natural instincts of justice, and refine its natural tact of love.

All such knowledge should be given her as may enable her to understand, and even to aid, the work of men: and yet it should be given, not as knowledge,—not as if it were, or could be, for her an object to know; but only to feel, and to judge. It is of no moment, as a matter of pride or perfectness in herself, whether she knows many languages or one but it is of the utmost, that she should be able to show kindness to a stranger, and to understand the sweetness of a stranger's tongue. It is of no moment to her own worth or dignity that she should be acquainted with this science or that; but it is of the highest that she should be trained in habits of accurate thought; that she should understand the meaning, the inevitableness, and the loveliness of natural laws, and follow at least some one path of scientific attainment, as far as to the threshold of that bitter Valley of Humiliation, into which only the wisest and bravest of men can descend, owning themselves for ever children, gathering pebbles on a boundless shore. It is of little consequence how many positions of cities she knows, or how many dates of events, or how many names of celebrated persons—it is not the object of education to turn a woman into a dictionary; but it is deeply necessary that she should be taught to enter with her whole personality into the history she reads; to picture the passages of it vitally in her own bright imagination; to apprehend, with her fine instincts, the pathetic circumstances and dramatic relations, which the historian too often only eclipses by his reasoning, and disconnects by his arrangement: it is for her to trace the hidden equities of divine reward, and catch sight, through the darkness, of the fateful threads of woven fire that connect error with its retribution. But, chiefly of all, she is to be taught to extend the limits of her sympathy with respect to that history which is being for ever determined, as the moments pass in which she draws her peaceful breath; and to the contemporary calamity which, were it but rightly mourned by her, would recur no more hereafter. She is to exercise herself in imagining what would be the effects upon her mind and conduct, if she were daily brought into the presence of the suffering which is not the less real because shut from her sight. She is to be taught somewhat to understand the nothingness of the proportion which that little world in which she lives and loves, bears to the world in which God lives and loves;—and solemnly she is to be taught to strive that her thoughts of piety may not be feeble in proportion to the number they embrace, nor her prayer more languid than it is for the momentary relief from pain of her husband or her child, when it is uttered for the multitudes of those who have none to love them,—and is "for all who are desolate and oppressed."

Thus far, I think, I have had your concurrence; perhaps you will not be with me in what I believe is most needful for me to say. There *is* one dangerous science for women—one which let them indeed beware how they profanely touch—that of theology. Strange, and miserably strange, that while they are modest enough to doubt their powers, and pause at the threshold of sciences where every step is demonstrable and sure, they will plunge headlong, and without one thought of incompetency, into that science in which the greatest men have trembled, and the wisest erred. Strange, that they will complacently and pridefully bind up whatever vice or folly there is in them, whatever arrogance, petulance, or blind incomprehensiveness, into one bitter bundle of consecrated myrrh. Strange, in creatures born to be Love visible, that where they can know least, they will condemn first, and think to recommend themselves to their Master by scrambling up the steps of His judgment-throne, to divide it with Him. Most strange, that they should think they were led by the Spirit of the Comforter into habits of mind which have become in them the unmixed elements of home discomfort; and that they dare to turn the Household Gods of Christianity into ugly idols of their own—spiritual dolls, for them to dress according to their caprice; and from which their husbands must turn away in grieved contempt, lest they should be shrieked at for breaking them.

I believe, then, with this exception, that a girl's education should be nearly, in its course and material of study, the same as a boy's; but quite differently directed. A woman, in any rank of life, ought to know whatever her husband is likely to know, but to know it in a different way. His command of it should be foundational and progressive, hers, general and accomplished for daily and helpful use. Not but that it would often be wiser in men to learn things in a womanly sort of way, for present use, and to seek for the discipline and training of their mental powers in such branches of study as will be afterwards fittest for social service; but, speaking broadly, a man ought to know any language or science he learns, thoroughly, while a woman ought to know the same language, or science, only so far as may enable her to sympathise in her husband's pleasures, and in those of his best friends.

Yet, observe, with exquisite accuracy as far as she reaches. There is a wide difference between elementary knowledge and superficial knowledge—between a firm beginning, and a feeble smattering. A woman may always help her husband by what she knows, however little; by what she half-knows, or mis-knows, she will only teaze him.

And, indeed, if there were to be any difference between a girl's education and a boy's, I should say that of the two the girl should be earlier led, as her intellect ripens faster, into deep and serious subjects; and that her range of literature should be, not more, but less frivolous, calculated to add the qualities of patience and seriousness to her natural poignancy of thought and quickness of wit; and also to keep her in a lofty and pure element of thought. I enter not now into any question of choice of books; only be sure that her books are not heaped up in her lap as they fall out of the package of the circulating library, wet with the last and lightest spray of the fountain of folly.

Or even of the fountain of wit; for with respect to that sore temptation of novel-reading, it is not the badness of a novel that we should dread, but its over-wrought interest. The weakest romance is not so stupifying as the lower forms of religious exciting literature, and the worst romance is not so corrupting as false history, false philosophy, or false political essays. But the best romance becomes dangerous, if, by its excitement, it renders the ordinary course of life uninteresting, and increases the morbid thirst for useless acquaintance with scenes in which we shall never be called upon to act.

I speak therefore of good novels* only; and our modern literature is particularly rich in types of such. Well read, indeed, these books have serious use, being nothing less than treatises on moral anatomy and chemistry; studies of human nature in the elements of it. But I attach little weight to this function: they are hardly ever read with earnestness enough to permit them to fulfil it. The utmost they usually do is to enlarge somewhat the charity of a kind reader, or the bitterness of a malicious one; for each will gather, from the novel, food for her own disposition. Those who are naturally proud and envious will learn from Thackeray to despise humanity; those who are naturally gentle, to pity it; those who are naturally shallow, to laugh at it. So, also, there might be a serviceable power in novels to bring before us, in vividness, a human truth which we had before dimly conceived; but the temptation to picturesqueness of statement is so great, that often the best writers of fiction cannot resist it; and our views are rendered so violent and one-sided, that their vitality is rather a harm than good.

Without, however, venturing here on any attempt at decision how much novel-reading should be allowed, let me at least clearly assert this, that whether novels, or poetry, or history be read, they should be chosen, not for what is *out* of them, but for what is *in* them. The chance and scattered evil that may here and there haunt, or hide itself in, a powerful book, never does any harm to a noble girl; but the emptiness of an author oppresses her, and his amiable folly degrades her. And if she can have access to a good library of old and classical books, there need be no choosing at all. Keep the modern magazine and novel out of your girl's way: turn her loose into the old library every wet day, and let her alone. She will find what is good for her; you cannot: for there is just this difference between the making of a girl's character and a boy's—you may chisel a boy into shape, as you would a rock, or hammer him into it, if he be of a better kind, as you would a piece of bronze. But you cannot hammer a girl into anything. She grows as a flower does,—she will wither without sun; she will decay in her sheath, as the narcissus does, if you do not give her air enough; she may fall, and defile her head in dust, if you leave her without help at some moments of her life; but you cannot fetter her; she must take her own fair form and way, if she take any, and in mind as in body, must have always

> "Her household motions light and free
> And steps of virgin liberty."

Let her loose in the library, I say, as you do a fawn in a field. It knows the bad weeds twenty times better than you; and the good ones too, and will eat some bitter and prickly ones, good for it, which you had not the slightest thought were good.

Then, in art, keep the finest models before her, and let her practice in all accomplishments be accurate and thorough, so as to enable her to understand more than she accomplishes. I say the finest models—that is to say, the truest, simplest, usefullest. Note those epithets; they will range through all the arts. Try them in music, where you might think them the least applicable. I say the truest, that in which the notes most closely and faithfully express the meaning of the words, or the character of intended emotion; again, the simplest, that in which the meaning and melody are attained with the fewest and most significant notes possible; and, finally, the usefullest, that music which makes the best words most beautiful, which enchants them in our memories each with its own glory of sound, and which applies them closest to the heart at the moment we need them.

And not only in the material and in the course, but yet more earnestly in the spirit of it, let a girl's education be as serious as a boy's. You bring up your girls as if they were meant for sideboard ornaments, and then complain of their frivolity. Give them the same advantages that you give their brothers—appeal to the same grand instincts of virtue in them; teach *them* also that courage and truth are the pillars of their being: do you think that they would not answer that appeal, brave and true as they are even now, when you know that there is hardly a girl's school in this Christian kingdom where the children's courage or sincerity would be thought of half so much importance as their way of coming in at a door; and when the whole system of society, as respects the mode of establishing them in life, is one rotten plague of cowardice and imposture—cowardice, in not daring to let them live, or love, except as their neighbours choose; and imposture, in bringing, for the purpose of our own pride, the full glow of the world's worst vanity upon a girl's eyes, at the very period when the whole happiness of her future existence depends upon her remaining undazzled?

And give them, lastly, not only noble teachings, but noble teachers. You consider somewhat, before you send your boy to school, what kind of a man the master is;—whatsoever kind of man he is, you at least give him full authority over your son, and show some respect to him yourself; if he comes to dine with you, you do not put him at a side table; you know also that, at his college, your child's immediate tutor will be under the direction of some still higher tutor, for whom you have absolute reverence. You do not treat the Dean of Christ Church or the Master of Trinity as your inferiors.

But what teachers do you give your girls, and what reverence do you show to the teachers you have chosen? Is a girl likely to think her own conduct, or her own intellect, of much importance, when you trust the entire formation of her character, moral and intellectual, to a person whom you let your servants treat with less respect than they do your housekeeper (as if the soul of your child were a less charge than jams and groceries), and whom you yourself think you confer an honour upon by letting her sometimes sit in the drawing-room in the evening?

Thus, then, of literature as her help, and thus of art. There is one more help which she cannot do without—one which, alone, has sometimes done more than all other influences besides,—the help of wild and fair nature. Hear this of the education of Joan of Arc:

"The education of this poor girl was mean according to the present standard; was ineffably grand, according to a purer philosophic standard; and only not good for our age, because for us it would be unattainable. * * *

"Next after her spiritual advantages, she owed most to the advantages of her situation. The fountain of Domrémy was on the brink of a boundless forest; and it was haunted to that degree by fairies, that the parish priest (*curé*) was obliged to read mass there once a year, in order to keep them in any decent bounds. * * *

"But the forests of Domrémy—those were the glories of the land, for in them abode mysterious powers and ancient secrets that towered into tragic strength. 'Abbeys there were, and abbey windows,'—'like Moorish temples of the Hindoos,' that exercised even princely power both in Touraine and in the German Diets. These had their sweet bells that pierced the forests for many a league at matins or vespers, and each its own dreamy legend. Few enough, and scattered enough, were these abbeys, so as in no degree to disturb the deep solitude of the region; yet many enough to spread a network or awning of Christian sanctity over what else might have seemed a heathen wilderness." *

Now, you cannot, indeed, have here in England, woods ighteen miles deep to the centre; but you can, perhaps, keep a fairy or two for your children yet, if you wish to keep them. But *do* you wish it? Suppose you had each, at the

* "Joan of Arc: in reference to M. Michelet's History of France." De Quincey's Works. Vol. iii. p. 217.

back of your houses, a garden, large enough for your children to play in, with just as much lawn as would give them room to run,—no more—and that you could not change your abode; but that, if you chose, you could double your income, or quadruple it, by digging a coal shaft in the middle of the lawn, and turning the flower-beds into heaps of coke. Would you do it? I think not. I can tell you, you would be wrong if you did, though it gave you income sixty-fold instead of four-fold.

Yet this is what you are doing with all England. The whole country is but a little garden, not more than enough for your children to run on the lawns of, if you would let them *all* run there. And this little garden you will turn into furnace-ground, and fill with heaps of cinders, if you can; and those children of yours, not you, will suffer for it. For the fairies will not be all banished; there are fairies of the furnace as of the wood, and their first gifts seem to be "sharp arrows of the mighty;" but their last gifts are "coals of juniper."

And yet I cannot—though there is no part of my subject that I feel more—press this upon you; for we made so little use of the power of nature while we had it that we shall hardly feel what we have lost. Just on the other side of the Mersey you have your Snowdon, and your Menai Straits, and that mighty granite rock beyond the moors of Anglesea, splendid in its heathery crest, and foot planted in the deep sea, once thought of as sacred—a divine promontory, looking westward; the Holy Head or Headland, still not without awe when its red light glares first through storm. These are the hills, and these the bays and blue inlets, which, among the Greeks, would have been always loved, always fateful in influence on the national mind. That Snowdon is your Parnassus; but where are its Muses? That Holyhead mountain is your Island of Ægina, but where is its Temple to Minerva?

Shall I read you what the Christian Minerva had achieved under the shadow of our Parnassus, up to the year 1848?—Here is a little account of a Welsh school, from page 261 of the Report on Wales, published by the Committee of Council on Education. This is a school close to a town containing 5,000 persons:—

> "I then called up a larger class, most of whom had recently come to the school. Three girls repeatedly declared they had never heard of Christ, and two that they had never heard of God. Two out of six thought Christ was on earth now ('they might have had a worse thought, perhaps'), three knew nothing about the crucifixion. Four out of seven did not know the names of the months, nor the number of days in a year. They had no notion of addition beyond two and two, or three and three; their minds were perfect blanks."

Oh ye women of England! from the Princess of that Wales

to the simplest of you, do not think your own children can be brought into their true fold of rest while these are scattered on the hills, as sheep having no shepherd. And do not think your daughters can be trained to the truth of their own human beauty, while the pleasant places, which God made at once for their school-room and their play-ground, lie desolate and defiled. You cannot baptize them rightly in those inch-deep fonts of yours, unless you baptize them also in the sweet waters which the great Lawgiver strikes forth for ever from the rocks of your native land—waters which a Pagan would have worshipped in their purity, and you only worship with pollution. You cannot lead your children faithfully to those narrow axe-hewn church altars of yours, while the dark azure altars in heaven—the mountains that sustain your island throne,—mountains on which a Pagan would have seen the powers of heaven rest in every wreathed cloud—remain for you without inscription; altars built, not to, but by, an Unknown God.

III. Thus far, then, of the nature, thus far of the teaching, of woman, and thus of her household office, and queenliness. We come now to our last, our widest question,—What is her queenly office with respect to the state?

Generally, we are under an impression that a man's duties are public, and a woman's private. But this is not altogether so. A man has a personal work or duty, relating to his own home, and a public work or duty, which is the expansion of the other, relating to the state. So a woman has a personal work or duty, relating to her own home, and a public work and duty, which is also the expansion of that.

Now the man's work for his own home is, as has been said, to secure its maintenance, progress, and defence; the woman's to secure its order, comfort, and loveliness.

Expand both these functions. The man's duty as a member of a commonwealth, is to assist in the maintenance, in the advance, in the defence of the state. The woman's duty, as a member of the commonwealth, is to assist in the ordering, in the comforting, and in the beautiful adornment of the state.

What the man is at his own gate, defending it, if need be, against insult and spoil, that also, not in a less, but in a more devoted measure, he is to be at the gate of his country, leaving his home, if need be, even to the spoiler, to do his more incumbent work there.

And, in like manner, what the woman is to be within her gates, as the centre of order, the balm of distress, and the mirror of beauty; that she is also to be without her gates, where order is more difficult, distress more imminent, loveliness more rare.

And as within the human heart there is always set an instinct for all its real duties,—an instinct which you cannot quench, but only warp and corrupt if you withdraw it from its true purpose;—as there is the intense instinct of love, which, rightly disciplined, maintains all the sanctities of life, and, misdirected, undermines them; and *must* do either the one or the other; so there is in the human heart an inextinguishable instinct, the love of power, which, rightly directed, maintains all the majesty of law and life, and misdirected, wrecks them.

Deep rooted in the innermost life of the heart of man, and of the heart of woman, God set it there, and God keeps it there. Vainly, as falsely, you blame or rebuke the desire of power!—For Heaven's sake, and for Man's sake, desire it all you can. But *what* power? That is all the question. Power to destroy? the lion's limb, and the dragon's breath? Not so. Power to heal, to redeem, to guide and to guard. Power of the sceptre and shield; the power of the royal hand that heals in touching,—that binds the fiend and looses the captive; the throne that is founded on the rock of Justice, and descended from only by steps of mercy. Will you not covet such power as this, and seek such throne as this, and be no more housewives, but queens?

It is now long since the women of England arrogated, universally, a title which once belonged to nobility only; and, having once been in the habit of accepting the simple title of gentlewoman, as correspondent to that of gentleman, insisted on the privilege of assuming the title of "Lady,"* which properly corresponds only to the title of "Lord."

I do not blame them for this; but only for their narrow motive in this. I would have them desire and claim the title of Lady, provided they claim, not merely the title, but the office and duty signified by it. Lady means "bread-giver" or "loaf-giver," and Lord means "maintainer of laws," and both titles have reference, not to the law which is maintained in the house, nor to the bread which is given to the household; but to law maintained for the multitude, and to bread broken among the multitude. So that a Lord has legal claim only to his title in so far as he is the maintainer of the justice of the Lord of Lords; and a Lady has legal claim to her title, only so far as she communicates that help to the poor representatives of her Master, which women once, ministering to Him of their substance, were permitted to extend to that Master Himself; and when she is known, as He Himself once was, in breaking of bread.

* I wish there were a true order of chivalry instituted for our English youth of certain ranks, in which both boy and girl should receive, at a given age, their knighthood and ladyhood by true title; attainable only by certain probation and trial both of character and accomplishment; and to be forfeited, on conviction, by their peers, of any dishonourable act. Such an institution would be entirely, and with all noble results, possible, in a nation which loved honour. That it would not be possible among us, is not to the discredit of the scheme.

And this beneficent and legal dominion, this power of the Dominus, or House-Lord, and of the Domina, or House-Lady, is great and venerable, not in the number of those through whom it has lineally descended, but in the number of those whom it grasps within its sway; it is always regarded with reverent worship wherever its dynasty is founded on its duty, and its ambition co-relative with its beneficence. Your fancy is pleased with the thought of being noble ladies, with a train of vassals. Be it so; you cannot be too noble, and your train cannot be too great; but see to it that your train is of vassals whom you serve and feed, not merely of slaves who serve and feed *you;* and that the multitude which obeys you is of those whom you have comforted, not oppressed,—whom you have redeemed, not led into captivity.

And this, which is true of the lower or household dominion, is equally true of the queenly dominion;—that highest dignity is open to you, if you will also accept that highest duty. Rex et Regina—Roi et Reine—"*Right*-doers;" they differ but from the Lady and Lord, in that their power is supreme over the mind as over the person—that they not only feed and clothe, but direct and teach. And whether consciously or not, you must be, in many a heart, enthroned: there is no putting by that crown; queens you must always be; queens to your lovers; queens to your husbands and your sons; queens of higher mystery to the world beyond, which bows itself, and will for ever bow, before the myrtle crown, and the stainless sceptre, of womanhood. But, alas! you are too often idle and careless queens, grasping at majesty in the least things, while you abdicate it in the greatest; and leaving misrule and violence to work their will among men, in defiance of the power, which, holding straight in gift from the Prince of all Peace, the wicked among you betray, and the good forget.

"Prince of Peace." Note that name. When kings rule in that name, and nobles, and the judges of the earth, they also, in their narrow place, and mortal measure, receive the power of it. There are no other rulers than they: other rule than theirs is but *mis*rule; they who govern verily "Dei gratiâ" are all princes, yes, or princesses, of peace. There is not a war in the world, no, nor an injustice, but you women are answerable for it; not in that you have provoked, but in that you have not hindered. Men, by their nature, are prone to fight; they will fight for any cause, or for none. It is for you to choose their cause for them, and to forbid them when there is no cause. There is no suffering, no injustice, no misery in the earth, but the guilt of it lies lastly with you. Men can bear the sight of it, but you should not be able to bear it. Men may tread it down without sympathy in their own struggle; but men are feeble in sympathy, and contracted in hope; it is you only who can feel the depths of pain; and conceive the way of its healing. Instead of trying to do this, you turn away from it; you shut yourselves within your park walls and garden gates; and you are content to know that there is beyond them a whole world in wilderness —a world of secrets which you dare not penetrate; and of suffering which you dare not conceive.

I tell you that this is to me quite the most amazing among the phenomena of humanity. I am surprised at no depths to which, when once warped from its honour, that humanity can be degraded. I do not wonder at the miser's death, with his hands, as they relax, dropping gold. I do not wonder at the sensualist's life, with the shroud wrapped about his feet. I do not wonder at the single-handed murder of a single victim, done by the assassin in the darkness of the railway, or reed-shadow of the marsh. I do not even wonder at the myriad-handed murder of multitudes, done boastfully in the daylight, by the frenzy of nations, and the immeasurable, unimaginable guilt, heaped up from hell to heaven, of their priests, and kings. But this is wonderful to me—oh, how wonderful!—to see the tender and delicate woman among you, with her child at her breast, and a power, if she would wield it, over it, and over its father, purer than the air of heaven, and stronger than the seas of earth—nay, a magnitude of blessing which her husband would not part with for all that earth itself, though it were made of one entire and perfect chrysolite:—to see her abdicate this majesty to play at precedence with her next-door neighbour! This is wonderful—oh, wonderful!—to see her, with every innocent feeling fresh within her, go out in the morning into her garden to play with the fringes of its guarded flowers, and lift their heads when they are drooping, with her happy smile upon her face, and no cloud upon her brow, because there is a little wall around her place of peace: and yet she knows, in her heart, if she would only look for its knowledge, that, outside of that little rose-covered wall, the wild grass, to the horizon, is torn up by the agony of men, and beat level by the drift of their life-blood.

Have you ever considered what a deep under meaning there lies, or at least, may be read, if we choose, in our custom of strewing flowers before those whom we think most happy? Do you suppose it is merely to deceive them into the hope that happiness is always to fall thus in showers at their feet?—that wherever they pass they will tread on herbs of sweet scent, and that the rough ground will be made smooth for them by depth of roses? So surely as they believe that, they will have, instead, to walk on bitter herbs and thorns; and the only softness to their feet will be of snow. But it is not thus intended they should believe· there is a better meaning in that old custom. The path of a good woman is indeed strewn with flowers; but they rise behind her steps, not before them. "Her feet have touched the meadows, and left the daisies rosy." You think that only a lover's fancy;—false and vain! How if it could be true? You think this also, perhaps, only a poet's fancy—

> "Even the light harebell raised its head
> Elastic from her airy tread."

But it is little to say of a woman, that she only does not destroy where she passes. She should revive; the harebells should bloom, not stoop, as she passes. You think I am going into wild hyperbole? Pardon me, not a whit—I mean what I say in calm English, spoken in resolute truth. You have heard it said—(and I believe there is more than fancy even in that saying, but let it pass for a fanciful one)—that flowers only flourish rightly in the garden of some one who loves them. I know you would like that to be true; you would think it a pleasant magic if you could flush your flowers into brighter bloom by a kind look upon them: nay, more, if your look had the power, not only to cheer, but to guard them—if you could bid the black blight turn away, and the knotted caterpillar spare—if you could bid the dew fall upon them in the drought, and say to the south wind, in frost—"Come, thou south, and breathe upon my garden, that the spices of it may flow out." This you would think a great thing? And do you think it not a greater thing, that all this, (and how much more than this!) you *can* do, for fairer flowers than these—flowers that could bless you for having blessed them, and will love you for having loved them;—flowers that have eyes like yours, and thoughts like yours, and lives like yours; which, once saved, you save for ever? Is this only a little power? Far among the moorlands and the rocks,—far in the darkness of the terrible streets,—these feeble florets are lying, with all their fresh leaves torn, and their stems broken—will you never go down to them, nor set them in order in their little fragrant beds, nor fence them in their shuddering from the fierce wind? Shall morning follow morning, for you, but not for them; and the dawn rise to watch, far away, those frantic Dances of Death;* but no dawn rise to breathe upon these living banks of wild violet, and woodbine, and rose; nor call to you, through your casement,—call, (not giving you the name of the English poet's lady, but the name of Dante's great Matilda, who, on the edge of happy Lethe, stood, wreathing flowers with flowers,) saying:—

"Come into the garden, Maud,
For the black bat, night, has flown,
And the woodbine spices are wafted abroad
And the musk of the roses blown?"

Will you not go down among them?—among those sweet

* See note, p. 57.

living things, whose new courage, sprung from the earth with the deep colour of heaven upon it, is starting up in strength of goodly spire; and whose purity, washed from the dust, is opening, bud by bud, into the flower of promise; —and still they turn to you, and for you, "The Larkspur listens—I hear, I hear! And the Lily whispers—I wait."

Did you notice that I missed two lines when I read you that first stanza; and think that I had forgotten them? Hear them now:—

> "Come into the garden, Maud,
> For the black bat, night, has flown;
> Come into the garden, Maud,
> I am here at the gate, alone."

Who is it, think you, who stands at the gate of this sweeter garden, alone, waiting for you? Did you ever hear, not of a Maude, but a Madeleine, who went down to her garden in the dawn, and found One waiting at the gate, whom she supposed to be the gardener? Have you not sought Him often;—sought Him in vain, all through the night;—sought Him in vain at the gate of that old garden where the fiery sword is set? He is never there; but at the gate of *this* garden He is waiting always—waiting to take your hand—ready to go down to see the fruits of the valley, to see whether the vine has flourished, and the pomegranate budded. There you shall see with Him the little tendrils of the vines that His hand is guiding—there you shall see the pomegranate springing where His hand cast the sanguine seed;—more: you shall see the troops of the angel keepers that, with their wings, wave away the hungry birds from the pathsides where He has sown, and call to each other between the vineyard rows, "Take us the foxes, the little foxes, that spoil the vines, for our vines have tender grapes." Oh—you queens—you queens! among the hills and happy greenwood of this land of yours, shall the foxes have holes, and the birds of the air have nests; and, in your cities, shall the stones cry out against you, that they are the only pillows where the Son of Man can lay His head?

THE END.

AN INQUIRY

INTO SOME OF

THE CONDITIONS AT PRESENT AFFECTING

"THE STUDY OF ARCHITECTURE"

IN OUR SCHOOLS.

BY JOHN RUSKIN.

Read at the Ordinary General Meeting of the Royal Institute of British Architects, May 15th, 1865.

NEW YORK:
JOHN WILEY & SON, 535 BROADWAY.
1866.

THE STUDY OF ARCHITECTURE.

I SUPPOSE there is no man who, permitted to address, for the first time, the Institute of British Architects, would not feel himself abashed and restrained, doubtful of his claim to be heard by them, even if he attempted only to describe what had come under his personal observation, much more if on the occasion he thought it would be expected of him to touch upon any of the general principles of the art of architecture before its principal English masters.

But if any more than another should feel thus abashed, it is certainly one who has first to ask their pardon for the petulance of boyish expressions of partial thought; for ungraceful advocacy of principles which needed no support from him, and discourteous blame of work of which he had never felt the difficulty.

Yet, when I ask this pardon, gentlemen—and I do it sincerely and in shame—it is not as desiring to retract anything in the general tenor and scope of what I have hitherto tried to say. Permit me the pain, and the apparent impertinence, of speaking for a moment of my own past work; for it is necessary that what I am about to submit to you to-night should be spoken in no disadvantageous connexion with that; and yet understood as spoken in no discordance of purpose with that. Indeed, there is much in old work of mine which I could wish to put out of mind. Reasonings, perhaps not in themselves false, but founded on insufficient data and imperfect experience—eager preferences, and dislikes, dependent on chance circumstances of association, and limitations of sphere of labour: but, while I would fain now, if I could, modify the applications, and chasten the extravagance of my writings, let me also say of them that they were the expression of a delight in the art of architecture which was too intense to be vitally deceived, and of an inquiry too honest and eager to be without some useful result; and I only wish I had now time, and strength, and power of mind, to carry on, more worthily, the main endeavour of my early work. That main endeavour has been throughout to set forth the life of the individual human spirit as modifying the application of the formal laws of architecture, no less than of all other arts; and to show that the power and advance of this art, even in conditions of formal nobleness, were dependent on its just association with sculpture as a means of expressing the beauty of natural forms: and I the more boldly ask your permission to insist somewhat on this main meaning of my past work, because there are many buildings now rising in the streets of London, as in other cities of England, which appear to be designed in accordance with this principle, and which are, I believe, more offensive to all who thoughtfully concur with me in accepting the principle of Naturalism than they are to the classical architect to whose modes of design they are visibly antagonistic. These buildings, in which the mere cast of a flower, or the realization of a vulgar face, carved without pleasure by a workman who is only endeavouring to attract attention by novelty, and then fastened on, or appearing to be fastened, as chance may dictate, to an arch, or a pillar, or a wall, hold such relation to nobly naturalistic architecture as common sign-painter's furniture landscapes do to painting, or commonest wax-work to Greek sculpture; and the feelings with which true naturalists regard such buildings of this class are, as nearly as might be, what a painter would experience, if, having contended earnestly against conventional schools, and having asserted that the Greek vase-painting, and Egyptian wall-painting, and Mediæval glass-painting, though beautiful, all, in their place and way, were yet subordinate arts, and culminated only in perfectly naturalistic work such as Raphael's in fresco, and Titian's on canvas;—if, I say, a painter, fixed in such faith in an entire, intellectual, and manly truth, and maintaining that an Egyptian profile of a head, however decoratively applicable, was only noble for such human truth as it contained, and was imperfect and ignoble beside a work of Titian's, were shown, by his antagonist, the colored daguerreotype of a human body in its nakedness, and told that it was art such as that which he really advocated, and to such art that his principles, if carried out, would finally lead.

And because this question lies at the very root of the organization of the system of instruction for our youth, I venture boldly to express the surprise and regret with which I see our schools still agitated by assertions of the opposition of Naturalism to Invention, and to the higher conditions of art. Even in this very room I believe there has lately been question whether a sculptor should look at a real living creature of which he had to carve the image. I would answer in one sense,—no; that is to say, he ought to carve no living creature while he still needs to look at it. If we do not know what a human body is like, we certainly had better look, and look often, at it, before we carve it; but if we already know the human likeness so well that we can carve it by light of memory, we shall not need to ask whether we ought now to look at it or not; and what is true of man is true of all other creatures and organisms—of bird, and beast, and leaf. No assertion is more at variance with the laws of classical as well as of subsequent art than the common one that species should not be distinguished in great design. We might as well say that we ought to carve a man so as not to know him from an ape, as that we should carve a lily so as not to know it from a thistle. It is difficult for me to conceive how this can be asserted in the presence of any remains either of great Greek or Italian art. A Greek looked at a cockle-shell or a cuttle-fish as carefully as he looked at an Olympic conqueror. The eagle of Elis, the lion of Velia, the horse of Syracuse, the bull of Thurii, the dolphin of Tarentum, the crab of Agrigentum, and the craw-fish of Catana, are studied as closely, every one of them, as the Juno of Argos, or Apollo of Clazomenae. Idealism, so far from being contrary to special truth, is the very abstraction of specialty from everything else. It is the earnest statement of the characters which make man man, and cockle cockle, and flesh flesh, and fish fish. Feeble thinkers, indeed, always suppose that distinction of kind involves meanness of style; but the meanness is in the treatment, not in the distinction. There is a noble way of carving a man, and a mean one; and there is a noble way of carving a beetle, and a mean one; and a great sculptor carves his scarabaeus grandly, as he carves his king, while a mean sculptor makes vermin of both. And it is a sorrowful truth, yet a sublime one, that this greatness of treatment cannot be taught by talking about it. No, nor even by enforced imitative practice of it. Men treat their subjects nobly only when they themselves become noble; not till then. And that elevation of their own nature is assuredly not to be effected by a course of drawing from models, however well chosen, or of listening to lectures, however well intended.

Art, national or individual, is the result of a long course of previous life and training; a necessary result, if that life has been loyal, and an impossible one, if it has been base. Let a nation be healthful, happy, pure in its enjoyments, brave in its acts, and broad in its affections, and its art will spring round and within it as freely as the foam from a fountain; but let the springs of its life be impure, and its course polluted, and you will not get the bright spray by treatises on the mathematical structure of bubbles.

And I am to-night the more restrained in addressing you, because, gentlemen—I tell you honestly—I am weary of all writing and speaking about art, and most of my own. No good is to be reached that way. The last fifty years have, in every civilized country of Europe, produced more brilliant thought, and more subtle reasoning about art, than the five thousand before them; and what has it all come to? Do not let it be thought that I am insensible to the high merits of much of our modern work. It cannot be for a moment supposed that in speaking of the inefficient expression of the doctrines which writers on art have tried to enforce, I was thinking of such Gothic as has been designed and built by Mr. Scott, Mr. Butterfield, Mr. Street, Mr. Waterhouse, Mr. Godwin, or my dead friend, Mr. Woodward. Their work has been original and independent. So far as it is good, it has been founded on principles learned not from books, but by study of the monuments of the great schools, developed by national grandeur, not by philosophical speculation. But I am entirely assured that those who have done best among us are the least satisfied with what they have done, and will admit a sorrowful concurrence in my belief that the spirit, or rather, I should say, the dispirit, of the age, is heavily against them; that all the ingenious writing or thinking which is so rife amongst us has failed to educate a public capable of taking true pleasure in any kind of art, and that the best designers never satisfy their own requirements of themselves, unless by vainly addressing another temper of mind, and providing for another manner of life, than ours. All lovely architecture was designed for cities in cloudless air; for cities in which piazzas and gardens opened in bright populousness and peace; cities built that men might live happily in them, and take delight daily in each other's presence and powers. But our cities, built in black air, which, by its accumulated foulness, first renders all ornament invisible in distance, and then chokes its interstices with soot; cities which are mere crowded masses of store, and warehouse, and counter, and are therefore to the rest of the world what the larder and cellar are to a private house; cities in which the object of men is not life, but labour; and in which all chief magnitude of edifice is to enclose machinery; cities in which the streets are not the avenues for the passing and procession of a happy people, but the drains for the discharge of a tormented mob, in which the only object in reaching any spot is to be transferred to another; in which existence becomes mere transition, and every creature is only one atom in a drift of human dust, and current of interchanging particles, circulating here by tunnels under ground, and there by tubes in the air; for a city, or cities, such as this, no architecture is possible—nay, no desire of it is possible to their inhabitants.

One of the most singular proofs of the vanity of all hope that conditions of art may be combined with the occupations of such a city, has been given lately in the design of the new iron bridge over the Thames at Blackfriars. Distinct attempt has been there made to obtain architectural effect on a grand scale. Nor was there anything in the nature of the work to prevent such an effort being successful. It is not an edifice's being of iron, or of glass, or thrown into new forms, demanded by new purposes, which need hinder its being beautiful. But it is the absence of all desire of beauty, of all joy in fancy, and of all freedom in thought. If a Greek, or Egyptian, or Gothic architect had been required to design such a bridge, he would have looked instantly at the main conditions of its structure, and dwelt on them with the delight of imagination. He would have seen that the main thing to be done was to hold a horizontal group of iron rods steadily and straight over stone piers. Then he would have said to himself (or felt without saying), "It is this holding, —this grasp,—this securing tenor of a thing which might be shaken, so that it cannot be shaken, on which I have to insist." And he would have put some life into those iron tenons. As a Greek put human life into his pillars and produced the caryatid; and an Egyptian lotus life into his pillars, and produced the lily capital: so here, either of them would have put some gigantic or some angelic life into those colossal sockets. He would perhaps have put vast winged statues of bronze, folding their wings, and grasping the iron rails with their hands; or monstrous eagles, or serpents holding with claw or coil, or strong four-footed animals couchant, holding with the paw, or in fierce action, holding with teeth. Thousands of grotesque or of lovely thoughts would have risen before him, and the bronze forms, animal or human, would have signified, either in symbol or in legend, whatever might be gracefully told respecting the purposes of the work and the districts to which it conducted. Whereas, now, the entire invention of the designer seems to have exhausted itself in exaggerating to an enormous size a weak form of iron nut, and in conveying the information upon it, in large letters, that it belongs to the London, Chatham, and Dover Railway Company. I believe then, gentlemen, that if there were any life in the national mind in such respects, it would be shown in these its most energetic and costly works. But that there is no such life, nothing but a galvanic restlessness and covetousness, with which it is for the present vain to strive; and in the midst of which, tormented at once by its activities and its apathies, having their work continually thrust aside and dishonoured, always seen to disadvantage, and overtopped by huge masses, discordant and destructive, even the best architects must be unable to do justice to their own powers.

But, gentlemen, while thus the mechanisms of the age prevent even the wisest and best of its artists from producing entirely good work, may we not reflect with consternation what a marvellous ability the luxury of the age, and the very advantages of education, confer on the unwise and ignoble for the production of attractively and infectiously *bad* work. I do not think that this adverse influence, necessarily affecting all conditions of so-called civilization, has been ever enough considered. It is impossible to calculate the power of the false workman in an advanced period of national life, nor the temptation to all workmen to *become* false.

First, there is the irresistible appeal to vanity. There is hardly any temptation of the kind (there cannot be) while the arts are in progress. The best men must then always be ashamed of themselves; they never can be satisfied with their work absolutely, but only as it is progressive. Take, for instance, any archaic head intended to be beautiful; say, the Attic Athena, on the early Arethusa of Syracuse. In that, and in all archaic work of promise, there is much that is inefficient, much that to us appears ridiculous—but nothing sensual, nothing vain, nothing spurious or imitative. It is a child's work, a childish nation's work, but not a fool's work. You find in children the same tolerance of ugliness, the same eager and innocent delight in their own work for the moment, however feeble; but next day it is thrown aside, and something better is done. Now, in this careless play, a child or a childish nation differs inherently from a foolish educated person, or a nation advanced in pseudo-civilization. The educated person has seen all kinds of beautiful things, of which he would fain do the like—not to add to their number—but for his own vanity, that he also may be called an artist. Here is at once a singular and fatal difference. The childish nation sees nothing in its own past work to satisfy itself. It is pleased at having done this, but wants something better; it is struggling forward always to reach this better, this ideal conception. It wants more beauty to look at, it wants more subject to feel. It calls out to all its artists—stretching its hands to them as a little child does—"Oh, if you would but tell me another story,"—"Oh, if I might but have a doll with bluer eyes." That's the right temper to work in, and to get work done for you in. But the vain, aged, highly-educated nation is satiated with beautiful things—it has myriads more than it can look at; it has fallen into a habit of inattention; it passes weary and jaded through galleries which contain the best fruit of a thousand years of human travail; it gapes and shrugs over them, and pushes its way past them to the door. But there is one feeling that is always distinct; however jaded and languid we may be in all other pleasures, we are never languid in vanity, and we would still paint and carve for fame. What other motive have the nations of Europe to-day? If they wanted art for art's sake, they would take care of what they have already got. But at this instant the two noblest pictures in Venice are lying rolled up in out-houses, and the noblest portrait of Titian in existence is hung forty feet from the ground. We have absolutely no motive but vanity and the love of money—no others, as nations, than these, whatever we may have as individuals. And as the thirst of vanity thus increases, so the temptation to it. There was no fame of artists in these archaic days. Every year, every hour, saw some one rise to surpass what had been done before. And there was always better work to be done, but never any credit to be got by it. The artist lived in an atmosphere of perpetual, wholesome, inevitable eclipse. Do as well as you choose to-day,—make the whole Borgo dance with delight, they would dance to a better man's pipe to-morrow. *Credette Cimabue nella pittura, tener lo campo, et ora ha Giotto il grido.* This was the fate, the necessary fate, even of the strongest. They could only hope to be remembered as links in an endless chain. For the weaker men it was no use even to put their name on their works. They did not. If they could not work for joy and for love, and take their part simply in the choir of human toil, they might throw up their tools. But now it is far otherwise—now, the best having been done—and for a couple of hundred years, the best of us being confessed to have come short of it, everybody thinks that he may be the great man once again; and this is certain, that whatever in art is done for display, is invariably wrong.

But, secondly, consider the attractive power of false art, completed, as compared with imperfect art advancing to completion. Archaic work, so far as faultful, is repulsive; but advanced work is, in all its faults, attractive. The moment that art has reached the point at which it becomes sensitively and delicately imitative, it appeals to a new audience. From that instant it addresses the sensualist and the idler. Its deceptions, its successes, its subtleties, become interesting to every condition of folly, of frivolity, and of vice. And this new audience brings to bear upon the art in which its foolish and wicked interest has been unhappily awakened, the full power of its riches: the largest bribes of gold as well as of praise are offered to the artist who will betray his art, until at last, from the sculpture of Phidias and fresco of Luini, it sinks into the cabinet ivory and the picture kept under lock and key. Between these highest and lowest types, there is a vast mass of merely imitative and delicately sensual sculpture; veiled nymphs—chained slaves—soft goddesses seen by rose-light through suspended curtains—drawing-room portraits and domesticities, and such like, in which the interest is either merely personal and selfish, or dramatic and sensational; in either case, destructive of the power of the public to sympathize with the aims of great architects.

Gentlemen, I am no Puritan, and have never praised or advocated Puritanical art. The two pictures which I would last part with out of our National Gallery, if there were question of parting with any, would be Titian's Bacchus and Correggio's Venus. But the noble naturalism of these was the fruit of ages of previous courage, continence, and religion—it was the fulness of passion in the life of a Britomart. But the mid age and old age of nations is not like the mid age or old age of noble women. National decrepitude must be criminal. National death can only be by disease, and yet it is almost impossible, out of the history of the art of nations, to elicit the true conditions relating to its decline in any demonstrable manner. The history of Italian art is that of a struggle between superstition and naturalism on one side, between continence and sensuality on another. So far as naturalism prevailed over superstition, there is always progress; so far as sensuality over chastity, death. And the two contests are simultaneous. It is impossible to distinguish one victory from the other. Observe, however, I say victory over superstition, not over religion. Let me carefully define the difference. Superstition, in all times and among all nations, is the fear of a spirit whose passions are those of a man, whose acts are the acts of a man; who is present in some places, not in others; who makes some places holy, and not others; who is kind to one person, unkind to another; who is pleased or angry according to the degree of attention you pay to him, or praise you refuse to him; who is hostile generally to human pleasure, but may be bribed by sacrifice of a part of that pleasure into permitting the rest. This, whatever form of faith it colours, is the essence of superstition. And religion is the belief in a Spirit whose mercies are over all His works—who is kind even to the unthankful and the evil; who is everywhere present, and therefore is in no place to be sought, and in no place to be evaded; to whom all creatures, times, and things are everlastingly holy, and who claims—not tithes of wealth, nor sevenths of days—but all the wealth that we have, and all the days that we live, and all the beings that we are, but who claims that totality because He delights only in the delight of His creatures; and because, therefore, the one duty that they owe to Him, and the only service they can render Him, is to be happy. A Spirit, therefore, whose eternal benevolence cannot be angered, cannot be appeased; whose laws are everlasting and inexorable,. so that heaven and earth must indeed pass away if one jot of them failed: laws which attach to every wrong and error a measured, inevitable penalty; to every rightness and prudence, an assured reward; penalty, of which the remittance cannot be purchased; and reward, of which the promise cannot be broken.

And thus, in the history of art, we ought continually to endeavour to distinguish (while, except in broadest lights, it is impossible to distinguish) the work of religion from that of superstition, and the work of reason from that of infidelity. Religion devotes the artist, hand and mind, to the service of the gods; superstition makes him the slave of ecclesiastical pride, or forbids his work altogether, in terror or disdain. Religion perfects the form of the divine statue; superstition distorts it into ghastly grotesque. Religion contemplates the gods as the lords of healing and life, surrounds them with glory of affectionate service, and festivity of pure human beauty. Superstition contemplates its idols as lords of death, appeases them with blood, and vows itself to them in torture and solitude. Religion proselytizes by love, superstition by war; religion teaches by example, superstition by persecution. Religion gave granite shrine to the Egyptian, golden temple to the Jew, sculptured corridor to the Greek, pillared aisle and frescoed wall to the Christian. Superstition made idols of the splendours by which religion had spoken: reverenced pictures and stones, instead of truths; letters and laws instead of acts; and for ever, in various madness of fantastic desolation, kneels in the temple while it crucifies the Christ.

On the other hand, to reason resisting superstition, we owe the entire compass of modern energies and sciences: the healthy laws of life, and the possibilities of future progress. But to infidelity resisting religion (or which is often enough the case, taking the mask of it), we owe sensuality, cruelty and war, insolence and avarice, modern political economy, life by conservation of forces, and salvation by every man's looking after his own interests; and generally, whatsoever of guilt, and folly, and death, there is abroad among us. And of the two, a thousand-fold rather let us retain some colour of superstition, so that we may keep also some strength of religion, than comfort ourselves with colour of reason for the desolation of godlessness. I would say to every youth who entered our schools—be a Mahometan, a

Diana-worshipper, a Fire-worshipper, Root-worshipper, if you will; but at least be so much a man as to know what worship means. I had rather, a million-fold rather, see you one of those "quibus hæc nascuntur in hortis numina," than one of those quibus hæc *non* nascuntur in cordibus lumina; and who are, by everlasting orphanage, divided from the Father of Spirits, who is also the Father of lights, from whom cometh every good and perfect gift.

"So much of man," I say, feeling profoundly that all right exercise of any human gift, so descended from the Giver of good, depends on the primary formation of the character of true manliness in the youth,—that is to say, of a majestic, grave, and deliberate strength. How strange the words sound; how little does it seem possible to conceive of majesty, and gravity, and deliberation in the daily track of modern life. Yet, gentlemen, we need not hope that our work will be majestic if there is no majesty in ourselves. The word "manly" has come to mean practically, among us, a schoolboy's character, not a man's. We are, at our best, thoughtlessly impetuous, fond of adventure and excitement; curious in knowledge for its novelty, not for its system and results; faithful and affectionate to those among whom we are by chance cast, but gently and calmly insolent to strangers; we are stupidly conscientious, and instinctively brave, and always ready to cast away the lives we take no pains to make valuable, in causes of which we have never ascertained the justice. This is our highest type—notable peculiarly among nations for its gentleness, together with its courage; but in lower conditions it is especially liable to degradation by its love of jest and of vulgar sensation. It is against this fatal tendency to vile play that we have chiefly to contend. It is the spirit of Milton's Comus; bestial itself, but having power to arrest and paralyze all who come within its influence, even pure creatures sitting helpless, mocked by it on their marble thrones. It is incompatible, not only with all greatness of character, but with all true gladness of heart, and it develops itself in nations in proportion to their degradation, connected with a peculiar gloom and a singular tendency to play with death, which is a morbid reaction from the morbid excess.

A book has lately been published on the Mythology of the Rhine, with illustrations by Gustave Doré. The Rhine god is represented in the vignette title-page with a pipe in one hand and a pot of beer in the other. You cannot have a more complete type of the tendency which is chiefly to be dreaded in this age than in this conception, as opposed to any possibility of representation of a river-god, however playful, in the mind of a Greek painter. The example is the more notable because Gustave Doré's is not a common mind, and, if born in any other epoch, he would probably have done valuable (though never first-rate) work; but by glancing (it will be impossible for you to do more than glance) at his illustrations of Balzac's "Contes Drolatiques," you will see further how this "drolatique," or semi-comic mask, is, in the truth of it, the mask of a skull, and how the tendency to burlesque jest is both in France and England only an effervescence from the *cloaca maxima* of the putrid instincts which fasten themselves on national sin, and are in the midst of the luxury of European capitals, what Dante meant when he wrote, *quel mi sveglio col puzzo*, of the body of the Wealth-Siren; the mocking levity and mocking gloom being equally signs of the death of the soul; just as, contrariwise, a passionate seriousness and passionate joyfulness are signs of its full life in works such as those of Angelico, Luini, Ghiberti, or La Robbia.

It is to recover this stern seriousness, this pure and thrilling joy, together with perpetual sense and spiritual presence, that all true education of youth must now be directed. This seriousness, this passion, this universal human religion, are the first principles, the true roots of all art, as they are of all doing, of all being. Get this *vis viva* first and all great work will follow. Lose it, and your schools of art will stand among other living schools as the frozen corpses stand by the winding stair of the St. Michael's Convent of Mont Cenis, holding their hands stretched out under their shrouds, as if beseeching the passer-by to look upon the wasting of their death.

And all the higher branches of technical teaching are vain without this; nay, are in some sort vain altogether, for they are superseded by this. You may teach imitation, because the meanest man can imitate; but you can neither teach idealism nor composition, because only a great man can choose, conceive, or compose; and he does all these necessarily, and because of his nature. His greatness is in his choice of things, in his analysis of them; and his combining powers involve the totality of his knowledge in life. His methods of observation and abstraction are essential habits of his thought, conditions of his being. If he looks at a human form he recognises the signs of nobility in it, and loves them—hates whatever is diseased, frightful, sinful, or *designant* of decay. All ugliness, and abortion, and fading away; all signs of vice and foulness, he turns away from, as inherently diabolic and horrible; all signs of unconquered emotion he regrets, as weaknesses. He looks only for the calm purity of the human creature, in living conquest of its passions and of fate.

That is idealism; but you cannot teach any one else tha preference. Take a man who likes to see and paint the gam bler's rage; the hedge-ruffian's enjoyment; the debauched soldier's strife; the vicious woman's degradation;—take a man fed on the dusky picturesque of rags and guilt; talk to him of principles of beauty! make him draw what you will, how you will, he will leave the stain of himself on whatever he touches. You had better go lecture to a snail, and tell it to leave no slime behind it. Try to make a mean man compose; you will find nothing in his thoughts consecutive or proportioned—nothing consistent in his sight—nothing in his fancy. He cannot comprehend two things in relation at once—how much less twenty! How much less all! Everything is uppermost with him in its turn, and each as large as the rest; but Titian or Veronese compose as tranquilly as they would speak—inevitably. The thing comes to them so—they see it so—rightly, and in harmony: they will not talk to you of composition, hardly even understanding how lower people see things otherwise, but knowing that if they *do* see otherwise, there is for them the end there, talk as you will.

I had intended, in conclusion, gentlemen, to incur such blame of presumption as might be involved in offering some hints for present practical methods in architectural schools, but here again I am checked, as I have been throughout, by a sense of the uselessness of all minor means and helps, without the establishment of a true and broad educational system. My wish would be to see the profession of the architect united, not with that of the engineer, but of the sculptor. I think there should be a separate school and university course for engineers, in which the principal branches of study connected with that of practical building should be the physical and exact sciences, and honours should be taken i mathematics; but I think there should be another school and university course for the sculptor and architect in which literature and philosophy should be the associated branches of study, and honours should be taken *in literis humanioribus*, and I think a young architect's examination for his degree (for mere pass), should be much stricter than that of youths intending to enter other professions. The quantity of scholarship necessary for the efficiency of a country clergyman is not great. So that he be modest and kindly, the main truths he has to teach may be learned better in his heart than in books, and taught in very simple English. The best physicians I have known spent very little time in their libraries; and though my lawyer sometimes chats with me over a Greek coin, I think he regards the time so spent in the light rather of concession to my idleness than as helpful to his professional labours.

But there is no task undertaken by a true architect of which the honourable fulfilment will not require a range of knowledge and habitual feeling only attainable by advanced scholarship.

Since, however, such expansion of system is, at present, beyond hope, the best we can do is to render the studies

2

undertaken in our schools thoughtful, reverent, and refined, according to our power. Especially it should be our aim to prevent the minds of the students from being distracted by models of an unworthy or mixed character. A museum is one thing—a school another; and I am persuaded that as the efficiency of a school of literature depends on the mastering a few good books, so the efficiency of a school of art will depend on the understanding a few good models. And so strongly do I feel this that I would, for my own part, at once consent to sacrifice my personal predilections in art, and to vote for the exclusion of all Gothic or Mediæval models whatsoever, if by this sacrifice I could obtain also the exclusion of Byzantine, Indian, Renaissance-French, and other more or less attractive but barbarous work; and thus concentrate the mind of the student wholly upon the study of natural form, and upon its treatment by the sculptors and metal workers of Greece, Ionia, Sicily, and Magna Græcia, between 500 and 350 B.C., but I should hope that exclusiveness need not be carried quite so far.

I think Donatello, Mino of Fiesole, the Robbias, Ghiberti, Verrocchio, and Michael Angelo, should be adequately represented in our schools—together with the Greeks—and that a few carefully chosen examples of the floral sculpture of the North in the thirteenth century should be added, with especial view to display the treatment of naturalistic ornament in subtle connexion with constructive requirements; and in the course of study pursued with reference to these models, as of admitted perfection, I should endeavour first to make the student thoroughly acquainted with the natural forms and characters of the objects he had to treat, and then to exercise him in the abstraction of these forms, and the suggestion of these characters, under due sculptural limitation. He should first be taught to draw largely and simply; then he should make quick and firm sketches of flowers, animals, drapery, and figures, from nature, in the simplest terms of line, and light, and shade; always being taught to look at the organic actions and masses, not at the textures or accidental effects of shade; meantime his sentiment respecting all these things should be cultivated by close and constant inquiry into their mythological significance and associated traditions; then, knowing the things and creatures thoroughly, and regarding them through an atmosphere of enchanted memory, he should be shown how the facts he has taken so long to learn are summed up by a great sculptor in a few touches: how those touches are invariably arranged in musical and decorative relations; how every detail unnecessary for his purpose is refused; how those necessary for his purpose are insisted upon, or even exaggerated, or represented by singular artifice, when literal representation is impossible; and how all this is done under the instinct and passion of an inner commanding spirit which it is indeed impossible to imitate, but possible, perhaps, to share.

Perhaps! Pardon me that I speak despondingly. For my own part, I feel the force of mechanism and the fury of avaricious commerce to be at present so irresistible, that I have seceded from the study not only of architecture, but nearly of all art; and have given myself, as I would in a besieged city, to seek the best modes of getting bread and water for its multitudes, there remaining no question, it seems to me, of other than such grave business for the time. But there is, at least, this ground for courage, if not for hope: As the evil spirits of avarice and luxury are directly contrary to art, so, also, art is directly contrary to them; and according to its force expulsive of them and medicinal against them; so that the establishment of such schools as I have ventured to describe—whatever their immediate success or ill-success in the teaching of art—would yet be the directest method of resistance to those conditions of evil among which our youth are cast at the most critical period of their lives. We may not be able to produce architecture, but, at the least, we shall resist vice. I do not know if it has been observed that while Dante rightly connects architecture, as the most permanent expression of the pride of humanity, whether just or unjust, with the first cornice of Purgatory, he indicates its noble function by engraving upon it, in perfect sculpture, the stories which rebuke the errors and purify the purposes of noblest souls. In the fulfilment of such function, literally and practically, here among men, is the only real use or pride of noble architecture, and on its acceptance or surrender of that function it depends whether, in future, the cities of England melt into a ruin more confused and ghastly than ever storm wasted or wolf inhabited, or purge and exalt themselves into true habitations of men, whose walls shall be Safety, and whose gates shall be Praise.

www.ingramcontent.com/pod-product-compliance
Lightning Source LLC
LaVergne TN
LVHW021410110826
845150LV00007B/1856

* 9 7 8 1 4 2 5 5 1 1 6 5 4 *